# Praise for *Inclusive AF*

"Jen O'Ryan has given a gift to the diversity and inclusion community and anyone challenged to create and maintain an inclusive, welcoming work environment. Inclusive AF is often conversational in tone, sometimes funny, but always founded in science and experience that is both relatable and practical. Literally a quick, direct, and easily understood "field guide" for those aspiring to translate good ideas and intentions into meaningful and sustainable results."

—*David Feldman, Manager,
Supplier Diversity, Chevron Corporation*

"This is a book like no other I have ever read about Diversity & Inclusion. It takes an entirely different angle and approach than I've ever seen before. If you're looking for a totally different angle and approach, you want this book ... and you want to read it cover to cover! It's outstanding."

—*Diane Conklin, Complete Marketing Systems*

"I love *Inclusive AF!* This book is REAL, outshining other, sometimes dull books written in a monochrome business style. It's like sitting down with Dr. O'Ryan for a coffee. As an Inclusion & Diversity professional, I would have loved this book at the start of my journey, and highly recommend it to everyone on the path."

—*Brian Ballantyne, Senior Program Manager,
Inclusion & Diversity, Amazon*

"Inclusive AF unpacks in a clear, direct way the neuroscience and sociological dimensions of encountering difference in the workplace. The reader will gain a deeper understanding of what has shaped the lives of the LGBTQ+ people they meet both in regular life and, in particular, at work. This is an essential handbook for how to create a welcoming and sustainable work environment in which LGBTQ+ employees can thrive."

—*Pierre Bradette, LGBTQ+ Community Activist and Management Consultant*

"This one will remain in my go-to resource library. Inclusive AF! offers an attainable path for HR teams, to reconstruct the antiquated policies of passively handling humans as a resource, instead of as an investment to improved company environments."

—*Kym Adams, CEO, The Business Team*

"Reading this guide feels like finding that endearingly quirky expert who explains the complicated science in hero movies. Imagine having that character explain inclusion and diversity. I am more comfortable leading Inclusion and Diversity efforts with this book in hand."

—*Mia Rella, Finance Professional, Bank of America Merrill*

# Inclusive AF:
## A Field Guide for
## Accidental Diversity Experts

# Jen O'Ryan, PhD

Copyright © 2020 Jen O'Ryan, PhD. All rights reserved.

No part of this publication shall be reproduced, transmitted, or sold in whole or in part in any form without prior written consent of the author, except as provided by the United States of America copyright law. Any unauthorized usage of the text without express written permission of the publisher is a violation of the author's copyright and is illegal and punishable by law. All trademarks and registered trademarks appearing in this guide are the property of their respective owners.

For permission requests, write to the below address:

Jen O'Ryan
1752 NW Market Street, #212
Seattle WA, 98107

The opinions expressed by the Author are not necessarily those held by PYP Academy Press.

Ordering Information: Quantity sales and special discounts are available on quantity purchases by corporations, associations, and others. For details, contact the author at Jen@DoubleTallLLC.com.

Edited by: Caroline Davis & Nancy Crompton
Cover design by: Jonathan Nesan
Typeset by: Medlar Publishing Solutions Pvt Ltd., India

Printed in the United States of America.
ISBN: 978-1-951591-30-4 (hardcover)
ISBN: 978-1-951591-31-1 (paperback)
ISBN: 978-1-951591-32-8 (ebook)

Library of Congress Control Number: 2020917074

First edition, September 2020.

The information contained within this book is strictly for informational purposes. The material may include information, products, or services by third parties. As such, the Author and Publisher do not assume responsibility or liability for any third-party material or opinions. The publisher is not responsible for websites (or their content) that are not owned by the publisher. Readers are advised to do their own due diligence when it comes to making decisions.

The mission of the Publish Your Purpose Academy Press is to discover and publish authors who are striving to make a difference in the world. We give marginalized voices power and a stage to share their stories, speak their truth, and impact their communities. Do you have a book idea you would like us to consider publishing? Please visit PublishYourPurposePress.com for more information.

 PYP Academy Press
141 Weston Street, #155
Hartford, CT, 06141

# Dedication

This book is dedicated to change agents everywhere, and to the unique value of being seen. To those fighting battles that no one else knows about. To those mustering every ounce of courage to walk through the world as who they are. To those who leverage the position or privilege they have, and use it to elevate others, amplify voices, and instigate change. To those we've lost, and those who are still here. You belong.

> *"You are a child of the universe no less than the trees and the stars; you have a right to be here.*
> *And whether or not it is clear to you, no doubt the universe is unfolding as it should."*
> —Max Ehrmann, "Desiderata"

# Contents

*Acknowledgements*   xiii

*Introduction*   xv
Overview and Introduction   xv
Practical Application   xvii
Disclaimers   xx
My Origin Story   xxi

NARRATIVE
**What Happens When You Give Your Audience a Red Pen?**   1

CHAPTER ONE
**The Business Problem Being Solved**   5
Why the Focus on Inclusion and Diversity?   7
It Depends on Who, and How, You Ask   10
Reality in the Workplace   13

CHAPTER TWO
**Start Here...**   17
Why Inclusion and Diversity Initiatives Fail   17
Defining New Projects and Early Prioritization   21
Building the Framework   22

NARRATIVE
**An Architect's Confession**   29

## CHAPTER THREE
**Lived Experience**    31
What's Behind "The Letters"?    31
Why This Is Different    34

## CHAPTER FOUR
**Humaning (What You're Up Against)**    39
Managing the Brain During Change    39
Your Brain Is Lazy. Like "Sweatpants" Lazy    40
Cognitive Bias    42

## NARRATIVE
**Would You Like Some Discrimination with Your Coffee?**    49

## CHAPTER FIVE
**Seriously, What's Wrong with People?**    53
More Rationalizing Than Rational    53
Early Messages    56

## CHAPTER SIX
**Managing Humans Through Change**    63
Scary Movies: The Science of Fear and Change    63
Navigating Humans through Change    65
Ambivalents, Enthusiasts, and Resisters    66
Practical Application    73

## NARRATIVE
**Bringing My Full Self to Work, in High Heels or Comfortable Shoes**    75
Quick-Service Oil Change Gig, 1994    75
Auto Parts Store, 1995    77
Self-Employment and Business Networking, 2010s    77

### CHAPTER SEVEN
**Designing Inclusion** — 79
The Big Three — 79
Avoiding Exclusionary Goals — 82
What to Do When Your Company Gets Called Out — 84
Policy — 85
Disrupt the Industry—C'mon, It'll Be Fun! — 88

### NARRATIVE
**The Kids Are Alright** — 93

### CHAPTER EIGHT
**Implementation Doesn't Have to Be Scary** — 95
Understand the System — 96
Working Across Teams — 100
Avoiding Dumpster Fires — 102
Communicating the Change — 105

### NARRATIVE
**Dichotomous: Two Very Different Environments** — 107

### CHAPTER NINE
**Inclusion as a Daily Practice** — 111
The Power of Language — 113
Who's Down with OPP? (Other People's Pronouns) — 114
Policy Does Not Equal Practice — 116

### CHAPTER TEN
**Let's Wrap Things Up and Get to Work** — 119
Crawl, Walk, and Run Projects — 120

NARRATIVE
**Bruce (West Hollywood, 1985)** 125

CHAPTER ELEVEN
**Until We Meet Again ...** 129

*Glossary* 133

*References and Resources* 137

*About the Author* 141

# Acknowledgements

This has to start by acknowledging the individuals who have shared their stories with me. Your courage and candor with such personal experiences is humbling; I cannot thank you enough for allowing me, and now others, inside.

Countless thanks to my husband, Paul, for (mostly) respecting closed doors and focus time. For those other instances, I offer countless apologies for using profanity like it was glitter on a macaroni art project. You have talked me in from multiple ledges, opened more than one bottle of "writing juice", and listened no matter what. I love you. There will probably be another book; sorry for that in advance.

Ray, K'ai, and Sydney—thank you for being early readers and slogging through some very rough, rough drafts. It is no small task to cover all that ground, while also providing direct and honest feedback. You helped shape this work in multiple ways and it's very much appreciated.

To my parents, Wayne and Joanne, thank you for your relentless encouragement and showing us how to find good in the world. Lauren, my sister and original partner in crime, thanks for always having my back. Spencer, you are my light. I couldn't ask for a better son; the world Is a better place with you in it.

My friends and colleagues, you are amazing human beings. I am extremely grateful for your unwavering support along this journey. I could not have made it this far without you all.

I'd also like to thank Jenn T. Grace, founder of Publish Your Purpose. Your insights, and uncanny ability to make this all attainable, are greatly appreciated. The book and I are much better works because of your influence.

Thanks also to my doctorate mentor, Dr. Connie Fickenscher. I am extremely grateful to have been able to work with you. None of this happens without the integrity, commitment, and grit that you make seem so effortless.

An additional thank you to everyone (colleagues, partners, friends, 'accidental experts,' complete strangers) who helped shape my understanding of this ridiculously complicated, multi-faceted, and continuously evolving subject. Conversations spark ideas that can change the world in unexpected ways.

Lastly, I would like to acknowledge and thank that one, small, seemingly innocuous e-mail response in 2003 that sent me down this path I'm on today. Who dares, wins.

*"Hope will never be silent."*
—Harvey Milk

# Introduction

## Overview and Introduction

So, you've been asked to take on the role of managing Inclusion and Diversity (I&D) in your organization. Panic sets in. Where can you even begin with all of this?

First, congratulations!

Second, *don't panic*. Launching successful projects is all about setting the intention and breaking things down into manageable pieces. Everything can seem overwhelming when you're looking only at an end result. It's like developing a training plan, one step at a time, with contingency plans, and figuring out the general sequence in which activities need to happen. Running a marathon happens with a series of small tasks that are designed to build on each other.

My intention in all of this is to equip people who find themselves (or would like to find themselves) responsible for launching Inclusion and Diversity initiatives and managing culture change across their organization.

At the same time, I want to start changing your perception. About inclusion, yes, but also about the myriad ways people interact with change and how that taps into deeply ingrained beliefs. This is a place to learn about blind spots, expand your vocabulary, and reframe perspectives.

The truth is that designing and implementing cultural change is hard. It's also time consuming and expensive.

These are not the qualities that cause most executives to rush in, ready to sign checks and allocate resources.

Advertising a culture of inclusion is fashionable, but navigating the complexity and hard work of developing an inclusive culture... that's an entirely different conversation.

It used to be, years ago, that you could slap a rainbow sticker on your product or business and be seen as "inclusive" or "welcoming."

Employees, clients, and consumers are becoming more discerning about where to invest their resources. Whether it's time, money, or personal reputation through referrals, people want companies that align with their values and priorities before deciding to commit.

They also have to see themselves reflected in your brand. Not just symbolically but represented throughout their experience of the company, product, and service—the full life cycle.

Here's the kicker—they don't need you, you need them.

Employees will go where they are valued and feel safe being themselves. Consumers will do business with companies that create space for them and remove exclusionary barriers. If they have to contort themselves into a box just to do business with you—that only lasts until there is a viable alternative.

Welcome to the beginning of viable alternatives.

We'll get more into that later, but it's important to appreciate from the onset. Signaling inclusion is important, but companies need to have an end-to-end system of support as people show up at their door (or website).

## Practical Application

Designing your Inclusion plan is like watching the sun set over a calm ocean, then suddenly being exposed to everything happening beneath the surface.

All the chaos, beauty, and fish poop keeps the ecosystem in check, with growth so slow that it seems impossible... all of this is the opposite of calm.

Creating lasting change in any system depends on understanding how to keep all the elements in balance. Your job is to maintain the pH level and keep the fish from eating each other.

The content here is designed to meet business leaders and change agents where they are—whether that's getting "unstuck" and developing an action plan, designing new employee engagement strategies, or coaching people managers on using 'they/them' pronouns.

This book has three main components:

- Launching projects (concept to postdelivery activities).
- Managing humans through change (unconscious bias, fear of the unknown).
- Designing inclusive programs for a specific segment of the population (LGBTQ+ individuals).

Some areas of this book discuss the human elements of change in greater depth, largely because that's where even the most elegant of solutions fall off the rails. You don't need to be an expert in all things human, but you will need some 'behind the scenes' info in order to navigate people through change.

While the book follows a general arc, sections are designed to be non-linear. The intention behind this is twofold. First, each reader will be in a unique position—whether it's the type of change they want to create or level of understanding around supporting LGBTQ+ employees. The non-linear chapter structure is designed to meet each reader where they are.

Second, structuring the content in a non-linear fashion also allows readers to come back to this book later on. It's like when you drive out to a place for the first time; the next trip always offers new perspectives. Also, the trip seems shorter, because the first trek gives context on what to expect.

I can't tell you how many times I've read *The Stand* by Stephen King. The first time I was in the eighth grade. It was an extremely worn copy that had been passed down by someone's older sibling. It was such a good story that it stuck with me for years.

The next time I read it was in my early twenties. I found a less worn-out copy at a bookstore. It was the first time I'd actually seen the cover art. This copy didn't need to be passed along to the next eager middle-schooler, so I kept it over the years, across multiple moves, jobs, and versions of me.

As each version of me revisited this book, every character and storyline resonated differently. The words were the same—I was the one who had changed. My perceptions and interpretations of each situation were different.

Same thing with the content in this book. Each project, initiative, and experience with change management will shift your understanding. The information here will be the same—your interpretation and how you are able to apply it will be different.

This book also contains a series of personal narratives—brief glimpses into someone else's worldview or experience. Some are funny. Some are not. But they are real. As a culture of storytellers, it's through narratives that we design a shared reality. My hope in this is that you find connections with people you will likely never meet.

Of all the sections in this book, to me these narratives are the most important. Not just because they are powerful (they are), but because each narrative is a *witnessing*, having one's experience heard and made more real. Each one sheds light on stories that need to be told... stories that too often remain unheard by those in a position to instigate change.

Connecting through stories also allows us to slip into another person's perspective. People can see themselves as various characters in the story, creating space for the reader to relate to both the hero and the villain during different stages. At the same time, the narratives make space for experiences that may have never occurred to you.

Through storytelling, these narratives become the Trojan horse, smuggling in relatable vulnerability rather than soldiers.

You might be tempted to skip over some of them. They may feel too foreign and unfamiliar. It's true, these stories are not for you, but you do own learning from them. You own doing the work—examining the different actors in each story and reflecting where you see yourself in them.

Are these stories going to change your life? Maybe, but that's not really the point. Investing the focused time to read them—really read them—might make you see things a bit differently. This could tap into something you thought you'd forgotten. Or, perhaps, that you long since decided not to think about.

## Disclaimers

A few disclaimers before we start. This book is intended as a guide, not a definitive set of rules. I've done my best to substantiate with research and data, where available.

We all know someone who chain-smoked cigarettes and lived to be 100. This is not about anecdotes—it's about diving into the deep end of a shared experience that could be vastly unfamiliar. Your actual mileage may vary.

Second, you'll also notice what appears to be an inconsistency throughout the book. While I use the acronym LGBTQ+ across my work, in some places you will see LGBT or LGBTQ used instead.

This is related to which acronym was used in reference to someone else's (cited) work. Example, if a study or survey uses the acronym 'LGBT', that is what's reflected here as well. It's not for me to change an existing source created by another author. More details are provided in the ending reference section.

Last, there are generalizations made along the way. Each person's experience is uniquely their own, and our understanding is constantly evolving.

But research does allow us to generalize to an extent. So, while the information shared here is based on extensive research that crosses my professional, personal, and academic worlds, it is not an absolute, capital "T" truth that exhaustively covers every possible situation.

As a culture, we love slapping labels on things. Please don't. And don't use this book as a checklist. It's a guide to help you navigate—again, think of it as a starter kit.

Stick with me here, and things will start to make more sense in a few chapters.

## My Origin Story

When I was little, I wanted to be Speed Racer, desperately. For readers under thirty, 'Speed Racer' was an English adaptation of a Japanese anime called "Mach GoGoGo." The show was about, well, exactly what it sounds like; Speed Racer and his brother/archnemesis, Racer X. They raced cars, were quite fashion-forward, and someone had a monkey. (I know, right?!)

Anyway, when I realized that Speed Racer was not going to be a viable career option, I stumbled my way into the tech industry. It was the mid 1990s, and a very different time. You really could stumble into situations like that.

It turns out that what I was good at—and drawn to—was optimizing systems, groups, and processes. I liked taking apart things that weren't functioning well and then deconstructing, organizing, putting them back together, and moving on to the next one.

I learned a lot about the complexity of change.

During this time, I was responsible for launching new customer experiences, beta testing new devices, and negotiating policy changes. Essentially, I've invested the last 20-ish years to develop an understanding how people interact with technology, with change, and with each other.

What I've learned along the way is a few things. First is how to implement change when humans are involved and second, how to move people into lasting change.

Sadly, I never did figure out why Speed Racer had a monkey.

The reason I'm laying this out is to give you some context on my worldview. All of these experiences influenced the approaches and best practices that I outline in this book.

I've been involved with the LGBTQ+ community since... well, ever.

My advocacy in supporting LGBTQ+ youth started almost two decades ago, as part of a Community Advisory Board for a local nonprofit. The program, known as MPowerment, was a small subset of a Seattle-based organization, chartered to provide services and support resources for people living with HIV/AIDS in the local community. MPowerment was funded by grants and focused primarily on peer-to-peer outreach, as well as education on sexual health.

I became involved with community programs for LGBTQ+ youth. This is where I first heard of GSAs (gay-straight alliances, also referred to as gender and sexuality alliances) that provide peer support for LGBTQ+ kiddos and their straight/cisgender allies. Fantastic!

My first thought was *where was this when I was in high school? This is amazing.* Working with these kids, it was striking how their experience of walking through the world was so different from their straight or cisgender peers.

They had to think about things like coming out, hiding who they were, tamping everything down, feeling 'different' from everyone else, shifting between personas to keep themselves safe. None of this even occurred to most kids who weren't queer. And why would it? It's not something that gets talked about.

After working with the youth and staff over a two-year period, it became evident to me that there was a huge need for additional support resources, designed specifically to address the unique issues faced by sexual minority youth. The challenges faced by these kids were radically different than their straight and cisgender counterparts.

Eventually, I decided to go back for my PhD. At that time, I wasn't quite sure what it was going to look like. It's such a huge scary commitment. You need to be certain that this is really what you want to do, because you're going to be living with it for a very long time during the process.

I knew that I wanted to contribute somehow. I've always had the sense, and it was instilled very early on from my family, but primarily from my mom, that you have to give back. You have to change things where you can, and you have to affect people and make life better for people, even if you never know who they are. Whether that's leaving extra room in the parking space or buying coffee for the person behind you in line... finding your way to change the world, whatever that looks like.

When I decided to go after a doctorate, I knew that I wanted to do something that would affect change in the LGBTQ+ community, but I didn't know what that was. It really wasn't until about halfway through the program that it really crystallized for me.

And then there was another rash of suicides among queer youth.

Kids and adolescents who identified as (or were perceived to be) LGBTQ+ were killing themselves after being subjected to relentless bullying.

Kids were dying. Kids. They were not just dying: they were killing themselves. Kids as young as middle school taking their own lives. Deciding to commit suicide because of how the environment was reacting to their emerging queerness. And those kids who weren't dying, were struggling.

As I drilled into research available at that time, an underlying problem became evident. Nearly every study and article represented being LGBTQ+ as a risk factor. The research viewed one's identity as a contributing factor to the likelihood of negative outcomes.

However unintentionally, this perspective placed responsibility of harm on those who experienced it. Being who they were contributed to these increased rates—as if violence, exploitation, and internalized conflict were natural inevitabilities for queer people.

They were seen as complicit in harm rather than the recipient of it. Imagine walking through a world so hostile to your emerging identity that the current body of research views your existence in it as a risk factor.

And I realized, well, that's... wrong. We're looking at this the wrong way. Our queer kids are fine. They're fine. It's their environment—more specifically, the response of that environment—to these kids' emerging identities that exacerbates or mitigates risk. Or makes being LGBTQ+ no more controversial than being left-handed or hating cilantro.

The research I conducted in support of my dissertation explored environmental influences that contributed to healthy development later in life. I started with the idea that queer kids are no more at risk than their straight and cis peers, unless their environment tells them they should be.

Revolutionary, I know. Sit with that for a minute.

The findings and themes that resulted from my study indicated something that most people in the community could already tell you, if asked.

Messages from one's environment about what it means to be LGBTQ+ are very influential through all stages of human development. These early messages formed the first story that kids would use to interpret themselves in the world. They shaped each child's understanding about what it meant to be 'queer'.

This is not to assume the experience of growing up as LGBTQ+ is fundamentally bad or rejecting. Supportive influences, such as family and peer acceptance, can contribute to a lower risk of negative outcomes and mental distress.

Why are we talking about early messages and childhood here? Because, at one point, all of your employees, clients, and consumers were children.

Humans tend to replicate situations from childhood over and over until we die. Probably afterward as well, but that's difficult to substantiate. All of these unique messages and experiences shape the values that influence people's investment of time, energy, and resources.

Organizational cultures that are actively inclusive (*Inclusive AF!*) do more than just improve retention, productivity, and employee well-being. They cascade messages that affirm and influence change.

The same is true for representation, visibility, and inclusive workplaces.

So, let's get started.

NARRATIVE

# What Happens When You Give Your Audience a Red Pen?

I've had the fortune of working with amazing wealth management clients for the past 25 years. But it is just in the last five years that I have learned the most about myself and the impact of 'invisible diversity.'

While I work with everyone, I usually work with women who have had a big event—retired, husband has died, or recently divorced. In many cases, their financial advisor belonged to their husband and they want a fresh start with a person who understands that their needs can sometimes be different. That's always been my experience and I never had a reason to look at things another way.

A couple of years ago I was giving a speech on how women need to pay attention to estate planning, just like always. I talked to them about how men and women often interact with wealth differently. About planning around statistics, like how the husband can die 15 years ahead of a wife. And I didn't think anything of it.

As I was talking to this small group about wealth planning, I looked around and saw that some of the women weren't engaging. It suddenly hit me! I knew many of these women personally, and I realized that they were married to women or identified within the LGBTQ+ community.

I realized the case studies I had been using for 20+ years about husbands and wives no longer applied. To make it worse, the pictures of men and women and heteronormative language was glaring. My industry had forgot these women. I had forgot them.

Taking this as a learning opportunity, I brought these observations back to my progressive company. When I told my colleagues my story and asked them what they thought about this, we had our communal Aha! moment. We realized that while we had blazed trails in working directly with women, we had the opportunity to go further.

So, I gave the presentation again to another group of women, and this time I brought red pens with me (honest to goodness, red pens). I explained to them what happened previously: that I had given the presentation, but that it didn't quite work. Then I asked them the million-dollar question: would they helped me edit it? The response was quite amazing, and it wasn't because we had a group of women that were all in same sex marriages or relationships. This was a group of moms, grandmothers, sisters; women who knew someone for whom this new perspective would be important. It was an opportunity for them to say, "Hey, this is important to all of us."

We worked with marketing team and our researchers, creating something that was remarkable. It's not only remarkable that we have the ability to tailor our program and make a difference for our clients, but also in that it was really transformative for my own understanding. This experience gave me the courage as a line employee to continually ask myself and my company "Are we doing everything we can? Are we really listening and paying attention?"

Diversity and inclusion in the workplace isn't just about taking the required bias tests and going to cultural training sessions. It's about how you learn from your colleagues and clients. It's about seeing them for who they truly are. I am so grateful to the room of women who spoke up with body language; so grateful I had the wisdom that day to notice how they were experiencing me and listen to what they shared.

As I write this, we are living through an historic shift for women of color. This is another opportunity for me. I'm gaining the wisdom to listen.

—Andrea Grosso Kaempf, financial advisor to womxn and those not served by the traditional male broker

CHAPTER ONE

# The Business Problem Being Solved

Does your organization promote an inclusive environment? Are you sure? Did you ask anyone?

One of a company's biggest differentiators is their ability to predict the need of customers, while also creating a workplace where employees feel valued and seen.

Think about the amount of time and research invested in understanding consumer need for a product. Entire departments are focused on market research, implementation strategies, consumer mood and perception, etc. Does your company do the same due diligence for the efficacy of Inclusion and Diversity (I&D) programs?

Company culture, advertising, customer service representatives... all are opportunities to show that an organization genuinely "gets it." Or unintentionally blow it. No pressure.

Before we get too much further into the details, let's talk about what's at stake for businesses:

- LGBTQ consumers increasingly use a company's reputation on equity in purchasing decisions (CMI, 2018).

- 71% reported asking friends/family to not buy a product because the company is not LGBTQ-friendly (CMI, 2019).

- 76% of consumers surveyed indicated that more of their business will go to companies that support LGBTQ equality (CMI, 2017).

- 78% of these same consumers also tend to support companies that market to and support the LGBTQ community (CMI, 2017).

- In business, LGBTQ budget controllers indicated that a company's LGBTQ-friendly reputation plays a role in choosing one company over another when making purchases on behalf of their employer:
    - All or nearly all the time (8%)
    - Often (19%)
    - Sometimes (32%)

Defining the business problem being solved is where most people get stuck. Remember the calm surface of the ocean versus the chaos underneath? Right, things can spiral out when one considers the array of possible influences, unknowns, and ways that this could all go wrong.

That's when companies turn to metrics and reportable data—who doesn't love those? I'm a business major at heart; trust me, I understand the satisfaction of measuring things into oblivion. Unfortunately, this approach can lead decision makers to fixate on the concrete (frequency and percentages) rather than the abstract (daily experience of human employees, consumers).

Because then it's easy to point at metrics from an Organizational Health Survey and have leadership say, "Numbers bad, fix numbers!" Numbers are surprisingly easy to tweak; humans are squishy and difficult to quantify.

Relying on people to escalate instances of bad behavior will tell you how many of "x" were reported but give zero insight into the complexity of each situation and, most likely, zero information on what *isn't* being reported.

Results from an Organizational Health survey aren't the problem being solved; neither are numbers related to frequency and percentages. Numbers are just one, surprisingly subjective, data point from a limited, self-selecting population (more about this in later sections, I promise).

And remember, people are looking for more than marketing campaigns that say the 'right thing.' This is about internalizing culture change across the entire lifecycle of employee, client, and consumer relationship.

## Why the Focus on Inclusion and Diversity?

"Why focus on Inclusion and Diversity when we have a perfectly good _____ for that?" Fill in the blank with "policy," "HR department," "Employee Resource Group," or "marketing team."

Excellent question—why are you, or your company, considering the importance of I&D programs?

I ask for two reasons. First, because it's nearly impossible to solve a business problem without understanding why you think there is one. Or to design a solution if you know there is a problem, but those in the position to effect change aren't quite there yet.

Second, because what you feel are motivating factors could be very different from what others see as the driving force.

For example, if I believe the only reason to promote I&D is due to outside pressure, that's going to impact the amount of resources I'm willing to allocate. Maybe I'll support a marketing campaign or a float in the local Pride parade. Ticking off a participation box becomes the priority.

If I believe that I&D improves the workplace and outcome for everyone, my approach is more likely to focus on strategy and long-term cultural development.

In a study conducted by the Institute for Public Relations (IPR, 2016), respondents were asked why they believe employers emphasize I&D in the workplace.

Among employed Millennials, the top three responses were:

1. To make it a better place to work in general (38%)

2. To increase opportunities for all employees (31%)

3. To improve employee morale (28%)

That's so nice! All about making things better for everyone. Now let's look at employed Gen Xers:

1. To increase opportunities for all employees (27%)

2. Because of outside pressures (25%)

3. To make it a better place to work in general (25%)

4. To make themselves look better/Improve their reputation (21%)

Erm... what's happening here? Seriously? Why is "because of outside pressure" tied with "to make it a better place to work in general"? Kinda disappointed here, Gen Xers.

On to the Boomers! Employed Boomers responded this way:

1. To make it a better place to work in general (29%)

2. To make themselves look better/Improve their reputation (26%)

3. Because of outside pressures (25%)

Increasing opportunities for all doesn't even appear.

Both Boomers and Gen Xers appear to interpret their employer's promotion of these initiatives as a need for validation from those outside of the company, rather than to benefit the organization internally.

Sit with that for a minute. Over half of respondents in the two older cohorts believe their employer emphasizes Inclusion and Diversity programs for reasons other than good humaning.

Maybe this is coming from a place of cynicism. Maybe it's based on previous experience. Either way, if this is what the employees are observing, imagine your target consumer's perception.

Full disclosure, this study has limitations, primarily a small sample size (1,002 US adults, including 634 employed respondents). I decided to include this data as a reminder of how generational perspectives can influence the perceived value of I&D efforts.

OK, so now we have some insight around perceived motivating factors. More details about how to deal with these challenges will follow in later sections. Let's take a look at why people may or may not be aware of problems in the workplace.

Data from the same IPR study also shows a variance across generations, related to "seeing" different types of bias or discrimination in the workplace.

I use quotation marks with "seeing" because, yes, this is about observable behavior, but it also involves an element of (spoiler alert) interpretation. A key element of developing awareness to problems is understanding what influences would cause people to not "see" them.

Organizations that rely on the number of complaints or issues filed with their HR department are missing out on volumes of real data. People can witness the same event and experience it very differently for myriad reasons. We'll cover these complexities in later sections. Think of this more as the warm-up.

Now, back to that survey!

## It Depends on Who, and How, You Ask

Employees and Leadership could be seeing problems differently across the organization.

When asked to list forms of discrimination or bias respondents observed in the workplace, here are the percentages reported (top 5) by age cohort.

| Forms of Discrimination or Bias (Top 5) | Employed Millennials | Employed Gen Xers | Employed Boomers |
|---|---|---|---|
| Any of the Following | 69%* | 57% | 46% |
| Racial/Ethnic | 27%* | 21% | 14% |
| Gender | 23%* | 16% | 13% |
| Age | 22% | 15% | 16% |
| Sexual Orientation/ Gender Identity | 21%* | 14% | 9% |
| Job Type, Title, Occupation | 17% | 11% | 12% |

*Statistically significantly higher than other generations.

Keep in mind that bias or discrimination by age in this sense could include people not being taken seriously because they are younger (presumed to be less knowledgeable or experienced), as well as older (presumed to be less technically savvy or unable to learn new methods).

What sticks out for me is the steep drop-off by age cohort for discrimination or bias observed based on race/ethnicity, gender, and sexual orientation/gender identity.

There are a couple of things that could be going on here. One possibility to consider is that employees in younger cohorts have learned different rules about what constitutes bias in the workplace. Millennials were the first generation to grow up with gay-straight alliance clubs in school and a different portrayal of social roles in the media.

Generation X was the first to benefit from Title 9 protections, which initiated a slow progression against gender-based discrimination in educational systems that receive federal funding. This cohort also grew up in the midst of a significant shifting of our national demographics. And, since Millennials are coming out more frequently than previous generations, Gen Xers have a higher likelihood of parenting openly LGBTQ+ kiddos.

Another way to pivot this info is to apply it against a typical leadership structure for organizations.

From a hierarchical perspective, if older employees have higher job levels (due to length of employment, years of experience, seniority in the role, etc.), that will cause a disproportionate cluster of them toward the top.

If it's true that younger employees generally populate more entry-level positions, or at least roles that don't shield them off in a corner office just yet, the day-to-day exchanges they observe between humans might be different.

Meaning that they are potentially exposed to a wider array of daily interactions, in ways that an executive or senior manager might not be. Essentially, most people avoid behaving badly in front of their boss's boss, more so than they would among peers.

Executives, managers, and others at the higher levels of companies likely have a very different perception of what's going on in the day-to-day lives of most entry-level employees.

Lack of broad exposure skews their awareness of an inclusion problem. Combine that with the perception that I&D programs are only emphasized because of outside pressures and—BAM!—there's your first business problem to solve.

People with the most leverage to influence, fund, and sponsor long-term culture change are potentially the least likely to be champions of it.

And that's where you come in.

## Reality in the Workplace

We've all seen the studies on the positive influence of diverse teams on innovation, problem solving, and more optimal outcomes. If you haven't, there are a few examples in the "References and Resources" chapter.

> "How Diverse Leadership Teams Boost Innovation". (BCG, 2018)

> "Diverse Teams Feel Less Comfortable—and That's Why They Perform Better." (HBR, 2016)

> "What makes a high-performing team? The answer may surprise you." (MIT, 2017)

The challenge is that to get these results, a couple of things also need to be present. People need to feel safe and able to show up as themselves. Teams have to create a trusted environment where unique perspectives are valued.

Time, energy, and the mental bandwidth invested in survival takes a dramatic toll on humans. Innovation takes a backseat to survival and staying intact.

In their "Cost of the Closet and Rewards of Inclusion" study, the Human Rights Campaign Foundation explored the impact of work environments for LGBTQ individuals (HRC, 2014).

Within organizations that were unwelcoming, respondents reported:

- Having to:
    - Avoid certain people at work (27%)
    - Lie about their personal lives (35%)
- Feeling exhausted from hiding their:
    - Gender identity (15%) or
    - Sexual orientation (20%)

In the 2018 Workplace Climate Survey, more than half of LGBTQ+ participants reported hearing jokes in the workplace about lesbian or gay people at least once in a while (HRC, 2018).

When respondents were asked why they didn't report incidents, the most common reasons provided were "because they didn't think anything would be done about it" and "because they don't want to hurt their relationships with coworkers" (HRC, 2018).

Considering the stigma associated with being LGBTQ+, and misconception that being LGBTQ+ is a "choice," many queer people have been socially conditioned to internalize responsibility for what others do to them.

A report published by the National Center for Transgender Equality indicated that more than 75% of gender diverse employees take steps in the workplace to avoid being mistreated (James et al., 2016).

Fifteen percent (15%) of these same respondents who had a job in the past year were verbally harassed, physically attacked, and/or sexually assaulted at work because of their gender identity or expression (James et al., 2016).

It's important to note that this survey is from 2015; the results were published in 2016. While that seems like a long time from a research perspective, not much has changed in subsequent studies.

Given these statistics, it's unsurprising that the same study indicated that nearly half of LGBTQ employees decide to remain closeted at work (HRC, 2018).

These realities are important for multiple reasons.

It's critical to understand that the experience of walking through the world as a queer person is very different. Exclusionary behaviors do not need to rise to a level of abuse in order to be harmful. Harmful not only to the person being targeted, but also to those who witness it.

Now that you're on this journey, I invite you to evaluate the profound exhaustion and drain on mental/emotional energy caused by unwelcoming workplaces.

On the surface, this exhaustion response can look like burnout or bad "group fit." In reality, the underlying issue is an environment that is unwelcoming to LGBTQ+ people. Subtle or overt, intentional or unconscious, these detrimental actions come with an incredibly high human cost and are preventable.

In situations like this, queer people are faced with an untenable decision: to hide this aspect of themselves or to come out, yet again, potentially facing a barrage of questions, discrimination, or threats to their personal safety.

People start at a new job, they put out family pictures, they fill out forms from HR, they typically send an intro email to others on the team.

All of this can be very different and scary if you have no idea how a picture of you and your same-sex spouse will be received. Or if your intro email lists your pronouns as "they, them, theirs."

As the new Inclusion and Diversity expert, your role in this is to prevent people from having to choose between coming out again (it's exhausting) or going along with a company's assumption and putting the disguise back on.

CHAPTER TWO

# Start Here...

## Why Inclusion and Diversity Initiatives Fail

So, why do specific Inclusion and Diversity initiatives fail? The answer is a resounding "It depends."

Super satisfying, I know. Stick with me here.

Programs that have lasting impact on organizational culture are extremely fragile. Think of them as beautiful azaleas—so bright, bursting with potential. Right up until you get them home and then watch them suffer a prolonged death while you learn the difference between "moist" and "damp." Don't get me started with the cool humidity and using vinegar to repot them. I'm already stressed out by hypothetical plants that don't even belong to me.

OK, so now that your amazing projects are azaleas, the organization is the environment. But this isn't the end of the process; now you have to think about all the other influences that can cause your project to flail around on the windowsill or thrive and become an industry standard.

The type of industry, nature of the work environment, receptiveness to new information, department structures and resources—all of these elements will interact with your projects. And I haven't gotten to the spectacular messiness of dealing with humans.

Still there? It's fine, take all the time you need.

Let's take a step back and look at this differently.

As a consultant, I'm the person who is usually brought in when projects are going badly. It's not always pretty. I've seen some things. But as an outsider, I also have the benefit of objectively assessing where deliverables started to fall apart, which generally leads to how the initiative can course-correct.

It can be a little like Indiana Jones wandering through an abandoned temple, except instead of a map and bullwhip, you get stale exports from MS Project and endless SharePoint lists (SharePoint... why'd it have to be SharePoint?). Reading through project outlines and schedules will reveal a great deal about the team, its priorities, and the ability to predict outcomes.

Over the years I've categorized some of the key elements of initiatives that either completely went off the rails or fizzled out in the first six months, never to see the light of day.

If you are familiar with managing projects, this list can look like overall best practices. To a certain extent, these points can be applied to launching projects in general.

But I&D projects tend to be different. They introduce changes that can be emotionally charged, and people may avoid talking about why they feel resistant.

It's also incredibly easy to do this wrong. And "wrong" in this case has a potential for unbelievably bad outcomes. Wish there was an easier way to describe it. You're dealing with humans: it's going to get messy.

So, here are the common themes I've observed in I&D projects that struggle. Most will have at least two, but usually three or four, issues that are intertwined. Projects suffer from:

- Lack of resources and focused expertise.
- Being defined without the context of lived experience.
- Intended outcomes or goals that are not realistic or clearly defined.
- Measuring that causes (or creates incentive for) undesired behaviors.
- Lack of proper (empathetic) motivation, understanding, and commitment from leadership.
- Cynicism among employees—lack of information, not internalizing this as a culture shift and need for innovation.
- Too much, too fast—saturation and change fatigue (allow soak time).
- Lack of follow-through (it's all in the follow-through).

It can be tricky to tease out individual problems. There are a lot of issues that can show up disguised as others. For example, a lack of resources can indicate a root problem that stems from cynicism and a lack of commitment or understanding from leadership.

One approach to help identify different influences is to expand each of these elements. Again, this will largely depend on your organization. Don't fixate on capturing everything. Start with a few points that you can come back to later.

For example, explore the following issues.

## Lack of Resources and Focused Expertise

You might be a seasoned expert on how the organization operates and getting things done, but you also might:

- Be too close and lack objectivity.
- Be too far removed and need deeper understanding of one-on-one team dynamics.
- Not have enough expertise in the subject matter or how to implement lasting change.
- Not have the capacity (or desire) to implement I&D projects on top of your day job.

## Intended Outcomes are Not Clearly Defined

You've been tasked to improve organizational health metrics but:

- Is the specific problem understood?
- Does the population being served feel this is a problem? Are they interested in the proposed solution?
- What are the specific features that make this a negative experience or outcome?

As you're going through this exercise, keep in mind that companies tend to rely on a silver bullet solution to address Inclusion and Diversity. They leverage exceptionally talented employees within the organization to drive change, often on top of their existing responsibilities. Or maybe the employee will be a shared resource, working a percentage of time each week for a period of months.

All of which sets teams on the road to one, or many, of the problems outlined here.

See the Introduction re: *don't panic.*

## Defining New Projects and Early Prioritization

It starts with getting everything out, like on *Hoarders*. All of these amazing ideas need to migrate from your cluttered brain onto paper.

There are multiple reasons to start with this, but basically, keeping that many tasks in your head takes up a lot of room. Your mind is literally walking around on the ceiling-high stacks of newspaper and debris that comprise your ideas. Time to clean things out and create space.

The process of writing down these concepts also helps them become clear. And shareable.

They can be organized and fully developed or merged into similar ideas. The written version gives you a set point, as opposed to your mental map, which can fluctuate or (gasp) forget important connections between thoughts.

I tend to block out focus time for this process. It can also be effective to keep a stack of note cards around and write things down as they pop up for you. The point is to get it out of you and down on paper. It makes the ideas more real and less "Oh, crap, I still have to do_____." Fill in the blank.

List everything you're thinking of developing. Write it down (yes, I know, with a pen and paper). Creating a visual will help you organize thoughts into themes. This exercise will also show you any gaps or ideas that are still too raw. Keep everything. Think of ideas as a nice sourdough—some come out fully baked, others need to sit on a counter and bubble for a while.

Put the Post-it notes (or whatever works for your brain) on a wall. Now, pick three things you want to introduce.

They don't need to be the objectives you think can be solved, or that have already been funded. They could be completely basic or doughy—it doesn't matter. Pick three ideas that you want to introduce. We'll get to the specifics later.

Humans are not good at multitasking but committing to one quest can spiral people into the chaos of second-guessing. Choosing just three ideas is intended to get you focused without becoming overwhelmed.

Congrats! Achievement unlocked!

## Building the Framework

This section is designed to help you outline and organize all of those amazing ideas bouncing around in your head.

We'll also cover some basic strategies that can prevent churn and frustration later in the process. Keep in mind, projects tend to follow a cyclical, not a linear process. And there are multiple ways to get an outcome.

## Define and Get Clarity on Your "Why"

Ask yourself questions and outline thoughts as they come to you. It doesn't need to be perfect—you'll have time to refine things as new information comes in. The important part is creating a baseline, a place to start.

But really getting into the "why" is a critical aspect of achieving your goals. Are you working:

- To improve the daily experience for all employees?
- To reduce attrition at your company?
- To make the world slightly better for everyone?
- Because someone assigned this work to you as part of next year's goals?

All of these are viable reasons, but understanding what motivates the goal will help you push through when things are difficult.

### Pro tip

Keep your "why" close to you (all the versions; remember, not everyone is going to resonate on the same points). The same is true for any versions of your business justification.

### *Set your intention*

The first time I heard this expression was during a snowboarding lesson. The instructor was emphasizing the connection between a line of sight and direction of travel. Super helpful for avoiding trees, but also translates nicely into achieving goals.

Think of it as running a diagnostic test. Evaluate each thought, question, comment, and resistance as they surface. Start with the basics and move out from there.

Not sure what an intention should look like? Feel free to use this as a starter: "Designing meaningful change that solves an actual problem, or fills an actual gap, according to the population being served."

### *Outline your goals*

Think high level. Goals at this stage can be as basic as "Finish reading this book" or "Don't resign."

Goals definitely fall into a category labeled "It's the journey, not the destination." Yes, that sense of accomplishment is huge; but the process of becoming and mastery along the way lasts much longer. Anyone can show up on race day; you'll have put in all those pesky training miles that get to the finish line.

### *Build a plan*

Defining a plan has several benefits. It helps break down a large goal into a series of smaller tasks. You can measure progress along the way and make course corrections. The process of planning also helps you to get more specific and realistic about what can be accomplished.

The plan doesn't have to be perfect, but it does need to be captured in whatever form works best for you. I'm very visual, so having an outline posted in full view is more helpful than a list that is in a drawer somewhere.

### Define your ecosystem

People talk about group dynamics almost as if it's an element that simply exists. Here is a tree, here is a mountain, and over there is an accounting department that is impossibly bureaucratic.

Take a step back and look again.

That accounting department is a system of humans, and humans use group behaviors to order themselves.

So, if there is a law that defines the speed limit as 55 miles per hour, but everyone goes 85 miles per hour (and law enforcement ignores them), then 85 miles per hour becomes the norm. People driving 55 are seen as impeding the flow of traffic, or worse, creating safety hazards.

Your organization can have the best inclusion policies ever (*Inclusive AF!*)... but what are people actually doing? Inclusion lives in the daily experience and group norms. Understanding how people interact will help inform your plan, communication, and later implementation.

Map it out—things are better understood with a visual.

Your map does not need to be tidy or exhaustive. Keep in mind there is a lot of learning involved at this stage. Your understanding of the landscape will likely evolve as you get deeper into the details.

Use stick figures, color coded Post-its, whatever works best with your brain. The important point is to express your thoughts in an accessible form.

You are building a visual starting point to help you understand:

- What you can influence and what you can't.
- How teams, interpersonal dynamics, and office politics intersect (which will inform how you approach introducing change).
- Where people who are potential advocates and champions land (which will inform how you influence them).

Create a series of contingency plans. Remember that things are going to go wrong. There will be unexpected plot twists along the road to implementation.

Allow space for unexpected delays; people being out of the office; new managers or leadership due to a reorg, strike, or industry shutdown; a snowstorm; a pandemic; the zombie apocalypse... everything.

Then go back to the same exercise where you first started outlining projects and deciding to what accomplish. Dump everything out of your brain. This is going to make you feel like that scene from *A Beautiful Mind* where the walls of John Nash's office are covered with news clippings, photographs, and a confusing web made of yarn and pins.

That's OK.

It's OK because now ALL OF THAT NOISE is outside your head. Now it can be prioritized, organized, and dispatched.

All of those ideas, or fragments of ideas, have been clamoring inside your head, sometimes even blocking other ideas that need the spotlight.

This process also helps you build credibility. Part of bringing people along on the journey is helping them to see that the path is there.

Trust me on this, not everyone will have the same capacity to envision how things can be different. It's not a character flaw or value judgment (although it can be extremely taxing).

People interpret the world (and risk/reward of change) differently. Meaning that you have to be adept at describing the safety features that are available.

Keep it simple and don't go too far into the weeds or tactical details. People can get hung up on your scenarios and miss the larger picture. Or become fixated on a risk you've classified as low impact and question your judgment.

What you are actually demonstrating here is that you've thought things through objectively.

Finally:

- Peel back the "I'm just one person, what can I do?" feeling, which can contribute to inaction.
- Have a healthy amount of tension in your goals.
- Acknowledge growth and real progress.
- Remember it's better to start small—we'll discuss this more later.

NARRATIVE

# An Architect's Confession

I was trained as an architect and practiced as one until a few years ago. Architecture, contrary to popular belief, was (and in many ways still is) a conservative profession, the kind where men wear black all the time. It may have the appearance of being artistic, cool, and environmentally responsible. But it is made up largely of repressed straight white men, who keep designing and building the same thing over and over again. The second oldest profession in the world, it's an egotistical gentlemen's domain; think Thomas Jefferson, Frank Gehry, Frank Lloyd Wright, Howard Roark.

When I was going to college in a liberal city in the late '80s, I wasn't out, not totally to myself, and definitely not to others. My class was split equally between men and women. But when I finished graduate school and joined a professional office, the number of female staff didn't reflect that. In the US, only about 25% of registered architects are women. (There are many reasons for this, but the main one is the lack of work-life harmony which pushes young mothers away from the practice.) The "boys club" would dominate the profession while women would fade away, and those same men end up running the firms and get published as "starchitects."

In that environment, it was not easy to be out, as the firms, construction sites and real estate developers are full of machismo. But I did come out, around the time I was finishing graduate school. Most of the women in my class and at the office became great encouraging friends. Guys at the office didn't know what to do with me. Even worse in the construction trailer.

It was frustrating, so I got involved with the architects' professional organization in their local diversity efforts, and eventually became the national chair of the diversity committee. Our goal was to make the profession resemble the gender, racial, and sexual orientation make-up of our country. I feel like we failed—it's still a straight boys' club.

Luckily, a lot of my own clients were in the healthcare, hospitality, and tech sectors, which I found to be much more fun and open-minded environments. I never had to hide my sexual orientation amongst the nurses, hoteliers, and geeks. I could truly be my own bubbly self. One of my former clients eventually recruited me to work in a big tech company, to help design their offices. It was the first time I worked with so many LGBTQ folks. And with our own Pride float!

Last year, in World Pride NYC I marched in the parade with a contingent from my current tech company. It was a truly liberating experience. As an architect, I was cooped up in a men-in-black environment. In the tech world, I can be rainbow every day.

—CK, a recovering architect

## CHAPTER THREE

# Lived Experience

### What's Behind "The Letters"?

Most people are familiar with the acronym LGBT or LGBTQ, maybe even LGBTQ+. But, as with any combination of letters used to represent humans, it's important to understand what they mean and how we got here.

Each letter is meant to describe a segment of the population. Lesbian, Gay, Bisexual, Transgender, and Queer or Questioning (both are used). The + sign, when used, represents all the other gender identities and orientations.

The acronym is helpful in the sense that it provides an overarching category to describe a group of humans. That said, using LGBTQ+ is problematic in a couple of ways.

These letters, and corresponding words, are organized in a way that leads people to interpret them as mutually exclusive or interchangeable. Meaning members of this group are either L, G, B, T, or Q. And that's it. You are one of the five options.

We're trying to capture extremely complex and uniquely human experiences; then turn them into an acronym for ease of use across a generalized population.

Let me illustrate another way...

People often conflate sexual orientation or attraction (the "LGB") with gender identity (the "T").

> **LGB**TQ
> Lesbian, Gay, Bisexual, Transgender, Queer (or Questioning)
> (sexual orientation)

Lesbian, Gay, and Bisexual describe one's attraction or sexual orientation.

> LGB**T**Q
> Lesbian, Gay, Bisexual, Transgender, Queer (or Questioning)
> (gender identity)

Transgender describes a gender identity—the innate sense of one's gender. This is completely unrelated to one's attractions. And, transgender is only one of many gender identities.

> LGBT**Q**
> Lesbian, Gay, Bisexual, Transgender, Queer (or Questioning)
> (overarching)

Queer or questioning are overarching terms and don't necessarily correspond with a specific gender identity or attraction/orientation.

Another challenge with these acronyms is that they reflect only the more commonly known attractions and identities. Lesbian, gay, and bisexual aren't the only orientations or attractions: transgender is only one of many gender identities. It can't ever be an exhaustive list; someone's identity is always going to be left out when using acronyms.

LGBTQ can also shift focus to a series of letters; distracting from the more important conversation of inclusion, equity, supportive workplaces, etc.

### In summary...

**Gender Identity**—The innate sense of one's own gender. (Transgender, cisgender, non-binary, agender, gender-fluid, and so on.)

**Orientation or Attraction**—Describes one's patterns of attraction. (Gay, lesbian, asexual, bisexual, pansexual, and so on.)

Before you panic, being amazing at I&D does not require you to be an expert in all things related to gender identity or sexual orientation. Start with understanding that there are other ways of being, and how to make space. Learning is a journey, not a destination.

So, why do you need to know this? Because designing LGBTQ+ Inclusion and Diversity isn't a "one size fits all" model. As you start looking deeper into the daily experience of employees, clients, and consumers, stay mindful of the complexities at an individual level.

I tend to use the term *queer* for a couple of reasons. To me it's more inclusive—covering the multitude of ways of being and describing this uniquely human experience.

Queer also speaks to a fluidity of human experience, as opposed to a static assignment.

Fluidity in this sense does not mean that "it's a phase." Coming out as bisexual should not be considered a cozy rest stop on the road to Completely Gay City. Fluidity relates to an evolving understanding of who we are, and deeper reflection into how one chooses to articulate that innate (and exceptionally personal) sense of self.

A word of caution: "queer" is interpreted as a pejorative for some members of the community, especially if the user is perceived to be outside of the community.

Context is everything; generational, cultural, and situational influences will impact your message. While you are navigating this space, stay present and mindful to how terms are being perceived.

What I'm primarily using, for the sake of clarity throughout the book, is LGBTQ+ (the plus sign indicates the multitude of other identities).

## Why This Is Different

I'm often asked why this population is different. And why Inclusion and Diversity programs, specific to the LGBTQ+ community, are so important.

Other people are bullied, made to feel different, and under-represented; why is there a need for programs designed for this segment of the population?

I usually say, "It's different because it is." Which really isn't an answer that people can connect with and is completely unsatisfying. The data geek in me wants more.

So, I follow up with this: Growing up as queer is different. Walking through the world as a queer person is a fundamentally different experience. LGBTQ+ people have unique challenges and experiences that most people outside the community never have to think about. It simply never occurs to them.

As I mentioned in earlier sections, the research I conducted in support of my dissertation explored environmental influences that contributed to healthy development later in life.

Because my dissertation research plan included interviewing adult humans within this segment of the population, it required approval from the University's Institutional Review Board (IRB). The IRB initially had concerns about my proposed interviews with people whom they viewed as members of a "vulnerable population."

That is, until my mentor challenged the reviewers to explain why lesbian and gay adults with no recent experiences with depression or other disqualifying considerations would be considered more "vulnerable" than the general population. Then things got quiet. And my research plan was approved.

Finally, I was ready to conduct interviews with 10 adults. Each session started with the same open-ended questions; asking them to talk about their experiences growing up. To share whatever they felt was most relevant to their story.

These exceptionally brave and candid people ranged in age from 23 to late 40s (the interviewee wouldn't tell me his exact age). Eight were from the United States and two grew up in other countries (India and Netherlands).

The differences were evident; we're talking about people from across a broad generational and regional spectrum. Experiential context ranged from one person who grew up soon after the Stonewall riot and in the midst of the HIV/AIDs epidemic, to another who grew up with a gay-straight alliance in school and computers in their back pockets that connected them to a global community.

Differences primarily fell into two categories: early messages and beliefs about what it meant to be *queer* (the umbrella term I'm using, since there was a wide array of terms used, heard, or understood by participants) and the availability of supportive resources.

The first category, early messages and beliefs, mostly related to availability and accessibility to information, as well as strong memories of how being LGBTQ+ was represented to them (in movies, television shows, news programs, the community).

The second category, availability of support, dealt with significant differences related to availability of and access to supportive resources. This category included everything from people in their circle who were accepting to trusted services or programs available within the community (gay-straight alliances in school, similar groups).

But then there were the similarities. They were striking. There isn't another word for it... it was striking.

Although each narrative varied, similar points were consistent across most of the interviews: Feeling alone. Feeling isolated. Feeling as though a 'terrible secret' had just been uncovered within themselves, and no one must ever know.

Coming out, feeling like you are the only one who wasn't given the "straight" or "cisgender" memo; coming out again, listening to people argue about whether you should have equal protection under the law... did I mention coming out again?

Duality, feeling alone, feeling that there is something innately wrong with them. Like they have this exceptionally scary secret. Fear of discovery that can cause a visceral reaction.

And more than anything else, which factors influenced the depth to which each experienced these feelings? Having at least one supportive and affirming person in their lives. Understanding that each person had value and belonged.

Yes, these experiences are shared among all humans; but there is a greater depth to the experience when there is an internalized sense of difference, of othering, it is quite simply not the same.

Where being LGBTQ+ differs is that this bullying—sometimes even to the point of denial that you exist as a person—can expand across all elements of your ecosystem.

Imagine seeing strangers publicly debate where you can go to the bathroom. Or if you can serve in the military. Or if you can be fired for having a non-binary indicator on a driver's license.

Through all these social discussions, an entire segment of the population becomes stigmatized as "less than."

This is why it's different to grow up as LGBTQ+... because of the additional obstacles to overcome based on the premise of being in need of "fixing." Because of from believing (as kids) that they were the only people in the world who weren't straight or gender conforming. Because of having to learn very early on where and when it was safe to be themselves.

The complexity of shifting, feeling that they had to compartmentalize between lives, and constantly evaluating how the environment was responding to them... these are everyday experiences in walking through the world as a queer person, as a child or as an adult.

And these experiences are exhausting.

CHAPTER FOUR

# Humaning (What You're Up Against)

## Managing the Brain During Change

Most people remember (at least I hope it's most, otherwise I'm just hella old) the antidrug commercial from the 1980s that featured an egg being fried in a pan, with the voice-over: "This is your brain [visual of an egg]; this is your brain on drugs [egg frying in a pan.]" You get the point.

The intent of this ad was to demonstrate that being "fried" was not good for your brain. Efficacy aside, the message resulted in a series of memes and caricatures that continue today.

For the purposes of this section, I invite you to think of your brain as a different type of egg. A slightly less ambitious egg. There is no gentle way to say this. It's time to understand just how lazy your brain truly is.

Not just your brain—everyone's brain is lazy. Maybe lazy is too strong a word; it has a lot of social connotation. OK, let's go with "optimized for efficiency and expending minimal energy required to complete a task." Super.

For this section, think of your brain as Gudetama, one of my favorite characters created by Sanrio and a quintessential representation of your brain on "foisted change."

Gudetama's name originates from a combination of the Japanese phrase for 'lazy' and 'tamago' (egg). So, essentially, lazy egg.

First, how adorable is that? Second, yes, Gudetama is often considered to have depression or at least serious malaise.

Rather than debate that here, let's focus on the expert level of "meh" that Gudetama brings to new endeavors. That's your brain when it's being tasked with yet another thing to learn (or worse, unlearn and relearn).

### Your Brain Is Lazy. Like "Sweatpants" Lazy

Our brains are optimized to conserve energy.

To be fair, humans are inundated with way more information than we can effectively process. Our brains filter out most of it so it can focus on what's most important.

Unfortunately, that "most important" is subjective. It's also way more slanted to what makes us feel good about ourselves. Try Googling "tragic selfie-stick related deaths" sometime and you'll see what I mean.

Anyway, our brains constantly flip through various filters. It prioritizes incoming messages, fills in missing details, and assigns attributes based on very little information.

Largely these shortcuts are bad. At best, they're inaccurate.

Your brain fills in the blank using a simple formula:

> minimal information available + perceived risk of harm + most likely profile, based on previous life experience.

For example, the statement "It's a spider" evokes different mental images for Seattle me than it does for my Australian colleague. But then your brain takes things one step further (optimization!). It solidifies these filled-in details and can retain them to build a belief that that's how the event actually transpired.

We go about our daily lives without thinking much about why we do the things we do.

Ask someone why they start at one side of the grocery store instead of another. Sure, there will be some element of logic: avoiding crowded sections, product sections that aren't needed. But beyond that, things start to fall apart. We tend to navigate the grocery store a certain way because—wait for it—at some point we just started doing it that way. Now it's become a thing. And our brains will find infinite ways to defend that decision as the best one, because it's the one we selected.

The logic part of us makes decisions based on previous experience. Don't park under those trees because your car will get covered in pollen or sap. Perfectly reasonable and based on objective observations. Don't park next to a beater car with body damage because...

What reasoning did your brain come up with?

Don't park next to the beater car with body damage because the driver doesn't exercise due care and might bump your car? Or because the driver is likely poor and won't have insurance if they cause damage? Or because the driver might break into your car? Or maybe the driver is a huge, menacing person with a bad temper, and now you're worried about personal safety?

Or did you think it might be an ambitious youngling who volunteers at a cat shelter, when they aren't busy developing the next technical innovation in the garage of their modest home?

Or were you caught up in a wave of nostalgia, remembering your own shitty first car that could only be started using a screwdriver? (True story.)

So many things go into creating a mental image and justifying the decisions based on that image: your innate sense of security and agency in the world, your personal resilience, the amount of support in your early years (more about that later), the perceived significance of risk in making a bad decision, etc.

**Cognitive Bias**

Another brain hack centers on preferential treatment for certain types of new information. Just as the body is in constant flux to maintain itself within an established range, our sense of self tends toward keeping things 'normal.'

Perceptions, patterns of belief, early messages... the younger we receive them, the more deeply ingrained they are and the more resistant to new information we become. Worse, we tend to hang on to inaccurate information even after being presented with facts that contradict it (the continued influence effect).

Confirmation bias describes the human tendency to add credibility to information that aligns with what a person believes and diminishes that which contradicts it. Humans tend to search out and cling to information that reinforces an existing belief.

When presented with new information that challenges the preferred 'normal,' the brain switches gears and attempts to diminish this new information in order to preserve the initial belief (and your brain's integrity). We experience discomfort or tension.

Rather than deal with an internal conflict, these responses are typically redirected toward the person most closely associated with this new information.

There are several problems with this approach to processing.

George Carlin famously joked that people considered drivers going faster than them "maniacs" and those driving slower "idiots." Incredibly funny and accurate, but why does this phenomenon occur?

Because we are the hero of our own story; our thoughts, behaviors, and beliefs are how we frame 'normal.' It never, ever occurs to us that we are all some other driver's "maniac" or "idiot."

Remember the last time a friend posted something on social media that completely contradicted your beliefs?

Was your first reaction to ask how anyone could possibly believe such nonsense? Did that immediately throw them into your "maniac" or "idiot" category? It may have, depending how close you are to them, and if your 'normal' in this area is deeply rooted.

Developing a narrative around others based on our experiential profiles has more influence than we realize.

My favorite example of this occurred during a road trip from Seattle to Portland. It's an easy drive—leave Seattle and drive south in an essentially straight line for about 3.5 hours. I was driving while my colleague was on the lookout for coffee shops that might have drive-through service. Traffic was light and we had the benefit of using the carpool lane. ABBA was on the radio and no one had to pee yet. Life was good. And then...

Out of nowhere a driver cut me off to get around a cluster of slow-moving vehicles. I immediately turned to my passenger and shouted, "Did you see what that guy did?"

In the fleeting seconds of exposure and processing what had happened, my brain had developed a full profile of the driver. Complete with back story, right down to their intentions. I'd created a mental picture of their gender (guy, obvs), approximate age, hairstyle, career aspirations, hobbies, and struggles going all the way back to high school. Stutter... he had a bad one. Overcame it finally, but it did a number on his self-esteem, for sure.

All of these details resulted from one split-second glimpse of a car being operated with questionable judgment.

This process is part of the information your brain brings along with physiological responses needed to preserve the body when it perceives a threat. Signals travel through the central nervous system to ready your body for response.

In the same split second your muscles are firing, the brain informs everything with, "Gah! Here is a rough approximation of what I think we're facing!"

To shorten the body's response time, your brain conjures up the most consistent details associated with the threat. It creates a profile based on what was observed (context), and fills in missing details based on an amalgam of everything previously experienced (similar to the earlier example of how the word "spider" has a different meaning for my Australian colleague).

In this case, it's possible I've imprinted many experiences involving a driver with specific attributes. My brain did the math and surfaced up the most likely profile. The unknowable details (career aspirations, mad bowling skills, unresolved trauma from high school) are tidbits picked up somewhere along the way.

You end up with a narrative that includes a mix of what was actually observed and the brain's rough approximation of necessary (but missing) details. It's like our personal version of Robert Downey Jr. as Sherlock Holmes, except we're not that good. In fact, we're terrible.

Since our brains want to protect the ego (it takes energy to be wrong or make corrections to the algorithm), confirmation bias comes into play. Every time I was cut off by a driver matching the developing profile, my brain filed that nugget under "*Aha!* I was right!"

Drivers outside of the profile, but doing the same action, were rationalized away and filed at the bottom of "things to look at later." If I was the driver cutting someone off, my brain would cultivate an elaborate list of reasons to support that decision.

As humans, we do this constantly; often without discerning the source (observable reality versus our own mental overlay, or some combination of both).

And now for why this is important within the context of launching Inclusion and Diversity initiatives. Admit it, you thought I'd forgotten.

This same processing system holds true for people of different ethnicities, economic status, gender identities, orientations, etc. Your unconscious bias immediately begins to filter in favor of personal experiences and early messages. This is why it's critical to take a step back and differentiate opinions from observable facts. Easier said than done, I know.

Taking the example a step further, had that driver's behavior caused an accident, the narrative I created would likely have influenced my actual recollection of events.

Any reporting of the incident would have listed completely unsubstantiated attributes. Those attributes would have then been filtered again by the person collecting my statement, with details being enhanced or diminished based on their own confirmation bias.

Pretty soon the local news is doing a special segment on alarmingly high rates of accidents among former stutterers with feathered hair parted on the side. You're welcome.

So, how did we get this far from the topic of inclusion?

Ah, right... the brain. Again, the brain wants to protect its ego. Also, inclusion.

NARRATIVE

# Would You Like Some Discrimination with Your Coffee?

Seattle, early '90s

When I was a young man just starting out in the world, I had an experience that change my course. I was around 20 years old, a time you are supposed to feel invincible. I didn't. I was full of fear, escaping the truth that haunted me. I grew up in Los Angeles and made the bold choice to move to Seattle to start a new life where I knew no one, where I could be anyone and be someone new. I began working in a hotel, in the accounting office. I was responsible for making change and cashing out the daily tills throughout the hotel, from the front desk, the bar, restaurant, gift shop, and coffee stand.

I was very shy; most people at the time would have described me as sweet and kind. But in reality, I was hiding demons. I sensed that I might be gay, but this was the height of the AIDS crisis and there was a lot of fear and misinformation swirling around me. I was caught in a struggle to discover myself but at the same time felt trapped, like I couldn't act on my impulses. I was certainly in a state of denial and could not open the closet door.

Knowing no one in this new city, work was my social outlet. One day when I was making change for the barista at the hotel coffee stand, he asked me, "are you...?"

At first I didn't know what he meant. Then I felt surprised, how did he know my secret? He was flirtatious. I said nothing, but my heart was racing. I quickly gave him his change and got out of there. I'm sure that I was blushing. Anxiety, fear, and excitement played through my mind for the rest of the work day.

The next morning when I got to work, my supervisor was counting out my till. I asked if something was wrong and he looked at me with disgust. He said the General Manager wanted to see me in his office. I was not sure what I had done. When I knocked on the door and was invited in, I was shocked to see David, the barista from the coffee stand, was sitting there too. The day before, I had been so exhilarated by my conversation with David but I felt so much anxiety, wondering what my coworkers would think. Unbeknownst to me, my exact fears were playing out among my colleagues.

After our interaction, David had gone to the front desk and asked if anyone there knew if I was gay or not. Apparently David wanted to ask me out. As innocently as this all started, David's question at the front desk struck the match, and the flames of the workplace rumor mill spread like wild fire throughout the building.

Our General Manager ask me if the rumors were true. I felt overwhelmed with guilt and shame. I said I did not know and I started to cry. But he said, it did not matter, that it was a disruption, and "we do not want your kind here". David and I were both immediately fired and ask to leave, without any severance or recourse. I had never felt so humiliated.

I was sharing an apartment with a co-worker at the time, and when he got home he also asked me if the rumors were true. I didn't have a good answer for him. He also said that it didn't matter, that this would look bad on him, and that I "needed to find a new place to live."

My whole world was turned upside down, over a simple glance, a quick inuendo, and my coworkers' fear. My safety net was gone. It didn't matter whether I was or wasn't, just the perception that I could be gay was unacceptable at the time.

That moment truly changed the course of my life. I knew I needed to get informed and fight for justice. I signed up for college classes to become an entrepreneur. I felt that by working for myself, I could avoid being fired in such a horrible way ever again. I came out and went on to fight for our civil rights. I became a leader on several community non-profit boards, and even served as the Chair of the King County Civil Rights Commission.

I continue to fight injustice even today. To me, it seems like times have really changed and work environments are more inclusive. Their priority is working with talented people, and employees are able to bring their whole authentic selves to work, rather than hide who they are.

## CHAPTER FIVE

# Seriously, What's Wrong with People?

## More Rationalizing Than Rational

The following example is purely fictional. Any resemblance to my friends, colleagues, or acquaintances is 100% coincidental.

*Person 1:* I don't feel well.

*Person 2:* You're probably hungover; you drank too much last night.

*P1:* No, no I didn't.

*P2:* Yes, you did, I was with you. You drank 17 pints of beer.

*P1:* That's not much for a person my size. Plus, I ate dinner. It's probably food poisoning. I wasn't drunk.

*P2:* You consumed 17 pints of beer and passed out on the front lawn. It's not food poisoning.

*P1:* I was tired. It's an early symptom of food poisoning. I looked it up on the Internet.

*P2:* You were singing Taylor Swift songs incoherently and vomited in the azaleas.

*P1:* According to this article, azaleas can cause food poisoning. As soon as I'm feeling better, we should have them removed.

Again, there are several problems with this approach to processing information. Faced with the decision of admitting we overdid it and possibly looking foolish in the process, the brain goes into its "public relations" mode and creates spin.

People* struggle when confronted with evidence that they have caused slights or offense to another.

The asterisk is used here to flag a generalization. Yes, there are segments of the population that, for whatever reason, are incapable of empathy or of conceiving that other humans have value. The asterisk is intended to avoid "What about Ted Bundy"-isms and missing out on the bigger point.

So, people* struggle when confronted with evidence of causing slights or offense to another. We tend to maintain an internal belief that "I'm a good person, and good people don't do X." We will bend details into memories that are easier for us to accept.

Memories of observable behaviors can be skewed to fit a narrative as well. Did they really watch this person consume 17 beers?

Your intention starts to fill in gaps of what transpired. Avoiding any evidence that you may have caused harm, or defending what you *did* by explaining what you *intended*, needs to take a backseat while you commit to listening and processing. It's a tough one to overcome. Like having to sit on your hands while talking.

I've seen people (including myself) perform some amazing intellectual gymnastics in order to avoid the painful, awkward truth: the realization that we made assumptions, or acted poorly, based on a form of cognitive bias.

### In summary...

Facing the possibility that an assertion or central belief might be flawed leads to a couple of things (well, at least four):

1. Requires extra processing energy that the brain would rather conserve for "Animal Crossing."

2. Presents the potential that we are wrong about other things (stirs insecurity, creates uncertainty, requiring even more processing energy).

3. Creates an internal conflict in which we try to justify why we might have shown questionable judgment.

4. Results in digging up innocent azaleas rather than evaluating our own behavior or decision process.

Be aware of where your brain is taking shortcuts for you. If you notice a tendency to reject a new data point or piece of information, take a moment and ask yourself why. Stay mindful of not only your mental response, but also any emotional or physical reaction.

Now let's look at where these filters come from in the first place.

## Early Messages

Think about the first messages you received about being different. Maybe not just different... about being 'other.' About groups of people who weren't like you.

Think about the first messages you received about identity. Gender, socioeconomic status, ethnicity, occupation, country of origin, sexual orientation... each of these come with associated expectations. It's part of our internal filtering systems that determine 'normal.'

As I mentioned earlier, we're going to bring this back to childhood occasionally, because:

- At one point, all of your employees, clients, and customers were children.
- Humans have a tendency to replicate situations over and over and over from childhood until we die. Probably after as well, but that's difficult to substantiate.
- Early messages are so deeply ingrained that we are rarely aware they exist.

Early messages do this for us:

1. They form a baseline for our 'normal' and help us contextualize new information.

2. They typically start with the people in our immediate circle (home, family) and can be amplified or diminished by secondary messages (community, school, peers).

3. They shape how we think of strangers, our response patterns, family norms, expected behaviors, and every person's role in various situations.

4. They can help keep us alive and safely navigate our environments, over which we have minimal control and yet feel ultimate responsibility for (childhood).

Most of us get our early messages starting at home. Parents, siblings, and family members all give us information about the world. How we should interpret ourselves as we walk through it. How we interact with others.

Our family of origin is more than the humans with whom we share history. They are our original programmers. Family of origin sets our threshold for what is 'normal.' It's not just about table etiquette and holiday traditions... like, the deep stuff. Family of origin establishes the capital "T" truth about subjective value in our world.

As children, we receive early messages about everything and develop an interpretation of reality based on these, plus our own experiences. Once internalized, these messages can be very difficult to change later in life.

We'll invest large amounts of mental energy attempting to discredit findings from that peer-reviewed, double-blind study if it doesn't jibe with what grandma always said about waiting 30 minutes between eating and swimming.

Double down on this if you've spent your entire life waiting 30 minutes and are a better person because of it.

That kind of internal conflict does not usually slip quietly into the night; it continues to cycle through an array of intellectual gymnastics until something sticks (see point 4).

Think of this as points on an *x-y* axis. "Zero" is our perception of 'normal.' 'Normal' is grounded in our interpretations of early messages, then influenced by our experiences and exposure to real life situations.

Our unconscious bias, informed by early messages, then pins things (ideas, people, behaviors) to points on the axis based on attributes and perceived value. When we're exposed to new information, and internalize it, our brain's interpretation of 'normal' either adjusts or is reinforced.

The more expansive our worldview, the more data we pull in to inform our filters. This is one of the many reasons I believe so strongly in travel. Not just the prepackaged, managed experiences (Disney, etc.), but actual deep travel. Travel that pushes you into someone else's experience of the world. To a place where you don't speak the language. Or can't interpret street signs (if there even are street signs, that is).

But I digress.

This is the framework of our belief systems. The early messages we receive tell us how to navigate safely, as well as what is expected of us. How to interpret ourselves, and others, out in the world. They shape our understanding of other people's positions in society, how they should behave, what their entitlements are.

## *Huge oversimplification alert*

Think about it this way—each of us has a personal ecosystem shaped in part by early messages, and then influenced when combined with a unique blend of:

- The people with whom we grew up and the dynamics within the home.
- The community in which we lived during childhood and adolescence.
- The cultural or religious beliefs of the family.
- Where we grew up (urban or rural environment, UK or US, Atlanta or Seattle, etc.).
- The time during which we were born (1930s or 2000s).

You might be wondering why this is important or even remotely connected to LGBTQ+ inclusion.

Excellent question. Here's the answer:

Your organization is an ecosystem subsuming each person's system. Early messages that inform beliefs apply at the individual level, and at the workplace level. (Mind blown; I know. This book was totally worth it.)

Whether you are designing a program or addressing group dynamics, it's important to understand how all these factors converge. Personal ecosystems (early messages, generational cohort, rural or urban dynamics, cultural truths, social structure truths) all influence how one will interpret what's observed or experienced.

Everyone involved in a situation is interpreting it through the filters shaped by their own personal ecosystem. Their responses and reactions are also being informed by these same filters.

Stick with me here. Let's go back to our Person 1 and Person 2 example.

Early messages also provide the script we fall back on when confronted with conflicting information. We take our cues on how to respond to new information from the humans around us early on. Sit with that for a minute.

Still with me? Good. Now, combine all of this with what we all just learned about the shortcuts our brains take when making (and reinforcing) decisions made on faulty interpretations of information.

When we're presented with evidence of having caused offense, it creates an internal conflict (cognitive dissonance). Our brains can't manage two contradictory ideas, so it limbers up for spinning the story.

Those patterns of behavior and early messages that kept us safe and helped us navigate the world are now choreographing how we handle and resolve contradiction. ("I'm a good person and good people don't do 'X.'")

Person 1 is a good person and good people don't intentionally hurt others. So, if Person 1 makes fun of people who are queer, or is otherwise abusive, it's not uncommon for person 1 to justify this behavior as "a joke". Another common fallback position (intellectual gymnastics) is to put accountability for their abuse directly on queer people. Person 1 was "just kidding" or "expressing a belief" and believes that any distress queer people feel must somehow be their own responsibility.

Person 2 is a good person and wants to be seen as a team player. Person 2 also happens to be openly queer. So, when Person 1 mocks them and makes cutting remarks, Person 2 pretends to be OK with it. Even though they are dying inside and struggling to maintain. They have been dealing with this since ever. Safest thing to do is go along and hope it stops. Some days it becomes too much, and they call in sick to avoid it.

I realize things are getting pretty heavy here, but it's absolutely critical to understand the humaning aspect of change. Things are rarely what they appear to be on the surface.

CHAPTER SIX

# Managing Humans Through Change

## Scary Movies: The Science of Fear and Change

There is a lot of science behind scary movies and people who enjoy being scared in a controlled environment (varsity-level carnival rides, "haunted" house attractions, etc.).

The best part about seeing scary movies in a theater is the collective release of tension.

Think about it: the filmmaker spends an inordinate amount of time building tension. People start responding without realizing it. Shoulders come up, heart rates increase, breathing becomes shallow. Finally, the intensity of the scene breaks. And what happens? That's right—a huge, collective exhale from the audience.

Pay close attention next time—this is a thing that happens. I'm not talking about just super-ultra-gory, extreme slasher movies. Really good, dark, stick-with-you insidious scary movies can do it to you too. When the intensity ends and the scene cuts to a new location (sorry, no pun intended), listen for everyone to start breathing again. Deep cleansing breaths help us to transition from heightened arousal to a calm state.

Your reptile brain is either super happy and reaching for the popcorn or has already taken charge and run your body out the nearest exit.

The same principles apply to learning about substantial change in the workplace.

Because change is terrifying. And awesome. And your experience will depend on how you process, the degree to which it directly impacts you, and myriad other factors. Most people fall somewhere in the middle.

The critical difference in scary movie, or other risky adventures like rappelling down a building Batman-style, is that it's exposure in a controlled environment. The movie is an active choice, as is my continued exposure to it.

I'm opting for the mind-bending thriller of the year. I'm not signing up for anticipating my elevator suddenly dropping five floors.

Or how about experiencing turbulence (I think they're calling it "rough air" now; kids these days) when flying 37,000 feet over the ocean.

I'm not equipped to survive for several days floating on this seat cushion. I'm a germophobe; there is not enough hand sanitizer in the metroplex to undo what's been done to this unfortunate collection of mauve fabric and what I assume to be some kind of sponge. No idea how these cushions are made, but I am not putting my face onto one. Of that I can assure you.

I've seen too many movies about how this ends. The person sitting next to me in 14E is doomed because my backpack really was too big to fit under the seat in front of me. I just kinda put my feet over it in a weird way so the flight attendant wouldn't notice.

So, yeah, sitting in a theater or rappelling down a building wrapped in 17 layers of safety harness... that's a yes. Lack of control, feeling ill-equipped to manage, high degree of unknown... hard pass.

Now let's view this through the lens of culture change.

### Navigating Humans through Change

We know that workplace bullying and toxic cultures have negative effects by every kind of measure. But why then would they be so difficult to change?

People like to be comfortable. Change means applying energy with an unknown outcome (maybe it isn't better, and now I also don't understand how things work).

Even when operating in toxic or dysfunctional workplaces, people can resist change. They may be uncomfortable with their situation, but they understand it and know how to exist in it.

We surround ourselves with like-minded humans, connect to sources of information that support existing beliefs, and tend to reject any contradictions in the comments section. Normal is sustained.

The question becomes, how do we use facts to counteract cognitive bias and influence change?

Easy. We don't.

Seriously, it's ridiculous to assume we could overcome millennia of human hardwiring with facts.

People don't connect with facts—they connect with other humans. You want them to come along on the journey? They need to see the benefit on the other side of change.

## Ambivalents, Enthusiasts, and Resisters

Perceptions and belief systems of an individual—combined with their degree of power over and the investment in (or benefit they get) from maintaining the status quo—greatly influences their response to change. Or even their capacity to realize that the organization has a problem with Inclusion and Diversity.

A couple of things I want you to understand before we get started:

- Everyone is the hero of their own narrative.
- You are composed of a series of complex systems; most of which are grounded in maintaining stasis (your 'normal').
- When these systems sense a threat to stasis, specific functions are executed to protect 'normal.'
- No one wants to be told that everything they've ever believed is wrong, even if it is (trust me on this).

Each person will land somewhere along a bell curve from resistance to acceptance when it comes to LGBTQ+ inclusion. You're likely already aware of the enthusiastic supporters in your organization. There are probably an equal number of resisters—people who, for whatever reason, aren't having it. We'll talk about both segments later. For now, I want to start with those in the middle of our curve.

People land at places along this curve for myriad reasons. You're bumping up against a lot of things. Early messages, experiences, ecosystems—all of these factors influence how people interpret the changes you are creating.

Not everyone got the same early messages about what it means to be queer. More specifically, what queer people are entitled to (when did equal protection under the law become "special rights?") and the personal blame they are assigned for whatever happens to them (prejudice, inequity, violence, erasure, invisibility, stigma, bias, rejection, exploitation, abuse, etc.).

My sense (well, combined with extensive research) is that people are often unaware of—or too uncomfortable to explore—their internalized beliefs about the amount of access, visibility, protection, etc., that marginalized populations should receive.

Part of acknowledging that Inclusion and Diversity initiatives are necessary includes acknowledging the existence of a system that discriminates and puts this population at risk.

It also requires that people do the work of understanding their bias, where it came from, and lack of factual basis for their prejudice world view.

'Othering' is easier for people to promote when they can see it as coming in response to some outside influence, rather than from within themselves.

You have to factor all of the internal (and often hidden) baggage into your change strategy. This is not meant to discourage you—only to give you a full picture of the situation.

And that isn't to say that people can't be brought along. Or that change resistance only exists in the context of Inclusion or LGTBQ+ initiatives.

I can't think of a single implementation that didn't have its share of change resisters. Some more obvious than others. People can be so resistant to change that they'll (intentionally or through inaction) sabotage progress or success of any kind.

We called them "legacy systems." In the tech space, legacy systems refers to antiquated systems (in this case, antiquated ways of navigating the world), that are difficult if not impossible to retire (or to "sunset").

In change management terms, it's the few resisters who prevent change from taking root in a culture.

They can be policy influencers, decision makers, people working on the daily grind... they can show up at all levels. The sad news is that it takes only a few resisters to derail everything you've worked to create.

Another segment of the population falls into the 'enthusiastic advocate' category. The enthusiastic advocates are all on board. They see the value and want these changes to happen. It might not even be limited to LGBTQ+ inclusion; they could be all in for that, as well as making the culture better in general.

You could geek out with them all day on how amazing the org could be. This is great and you should do this, but don't get hung up here. Trust me, it's very enticing to hang with the advocates. They're fun. They're like-minded. You all 'get' each other.

See where I'm going here? Right. You need advocates and they need your phenomenal change management skills, but that's not enough.

You need diversity, both in perspectives and representation. Spend too much time focused on enthusiastic advocates, then change will happen faster than other people can absorb. Allow too much obstruction from the resisters and nothing will ever happen, except your eventual resignation.

This is when you target the *ambivalents*. *Bring me the ambivalents!*

For the purposes of this book, I'm referring to those in middle of our inclusion bell curve as 'the ambivalents.'

Ambivalents are those who haven't really needed to think about LGBTQ+ inclusion. As the term indicates—they are ambivalent to creating a more inclusive culture.

Maybe they think things are generally OK. Maybe they have mixed feelings about what inclusion looks like. Maybe they're tired of being told that they're doing it wrong. All the things.

The point is that you can flip them. Or at least you have a better chance at flipping them than you do with a resister. So, this is where you focus the early energy.

You're looking to expand the number of advocates in the org. Don't invest time and energy into change resisters right away; there's plenty of time and strategies for that later.

You—yes, you—need to make this relatable for the ambivalents. Rely on the fact that once an issue is humanized, it becomes more difficult to ignore.

And then we start to tackle the resistors.

## Steps to Undo Change Resisters

First, don't try to influence people by pointing out the flaws in their belief systems. If you are undermining the basic principles that someone has constructed an entire life around, it's likely they will slam the door or punch you right in the facts.

Start by talking. Find common ground. Try to appreciate the issue through their worldview. Remember, they are the hero of their story and you are only an ancillary character at best.

Second, don't fight fire with fire—cut off the fuel source instead. When you see misinterpreted or misrepresented information, look for an opening you can use to clarify. Find and reference the source document when you can.

This also gives you an opportunity to review and check if your own bias is active here. I think the kids refer to this as

"Check yourself before you wreck yourself," but I could be mistaken.

Last, pick your battles. Some discussions will not end well for either party. Know when to take a step back for your own safety and emotional or mental well-being.

## Conformity Works Both Ways

Toxic behaviors that are called out are less likely to take hold or be normalized in an active culture of respect and inclusion. Interrupting in the moment ("Why would you say that? Not cool...") can be surprisingly effective.

Often, the challenge is that people don't know how to respond. They might be afraid, stymied by shock, or uncomfortably waiting for things to pass.

Here's the trick. It takes practice. Responding in a way that disrupts the behavior is like building muscle memory. You need to do the reps.

## Normative Social Influence

Even if you haven't heard of it, you've most likely seen examples of normative social influence. This is the drive toward adapting our behaviors to conform to critical group norms.

Humans are safer as part of a group. Meaning that if a colleague or client refuses to use correct pronouns and direct reasoning doesn't work to persuade them, then peer pressure and group norms within the team can help break down the resistance. Don't manipulate or contribute to an increasingly more toxic (or dangerous) work environment, but understand the impact of a cohesive team grounded in mutual respect and value.

## "Unresolvable Stress" in the Workplace

One thing to keep in mind: not all change resisters can be saved. A colleague of mine uses the term "*epistemologically closed*," meaning people who, for whatever reason, simply are not receptive to new information.

This sense of being closed can be specific to certain areas (social change, structure), or a general rigidity of perspective across the board.

Specific to introducing an LGBTQ+ inclusion initiative, being epistemologically closed can be difficult to pinpoint. It could be rigidity in seeing queer people as 'less than.' It could also be an unfounded fear of somehow "losing something" (status, access, resources) if others are invited to the table.

At the end of the day, it's on them to figure it out. And doing the work to uncover personal bias or prejudice is not always pleasant. It's not your job to figure out their 'why.' It's your job to cultivate an inclusive culture that is welcoming to all.

On that same note, one thing I do hear a lot is "If we're supposed to be welcoming to all, why can't I express unsupportive views of LGBTQ+ people?" Really, fill in any traditionally marginalized population at the end of that sentence. Essentially, it's a loaded question on why intolerance isn't tolerated in your safe, welcoming-to-all, inclusive culture.

Here's why: like freedom of expression, there are limits.

I'm not here to change anyone's belief system; diversity of thought and perspective are necessary. As an atheist, I am entitled to have my beliefs grounded in science, research, and the lived experience. This does not mean I can go into work and tell my devoutly religious colleague that everything they believe is a lie based on ancient mythology.

My deeply held beliefs and those of my colleagues do not need to be aligned or reconciled in any way. Because neither is negating the other's humanity. We respect one another's values and experiences. Sure, people can be assholes. They microwave fish in the breakroom and don't wipe down machines in the gym. Not cool. But that's another book. We're here to talk about inclusion.

**Practical Application**

Working through change resisters or resistant-leaning ambivalents may occur in stages. These are a few strategies I've found to be effective:

- State the point plainly: everyone has a right to their own identity and human dignity.
- Go back to the concepts around bias and the tendency to diminish or reject new information that contradicts an existing belief.

- Watch for subtle but damaging behaviors that are framed as a work style or personality conflict. (Refusing to use pronouns, sabotaging progress, "But that's not my belief," etc.)

- Talk through why a specific change is making someone anxious. What is the root concern? Again, you may need to revisit this several times and peel back the 'whys.'

NARRATIVE

# Bringing My Full Self to Work, in High Heels or Comfortable Shoes

## Quick-Service Oil Change Gig, 1994

It was 1994 in a small midwestern town—not a banner time or place for lesbians, especially those who weren't trying to hide it. In fact, as a hyper-femme lesbian married to a butch woman and living in an insular, intellectual feminist community, I worked extra-hard to be even more out, to look more butch (or at least androgynous) than I was. I cut my hair super-short. I learned to walk with purpose and take up space when I sat. As Robin Williams so famously put it, I wore comfortable shoes.

My "aggressively out" look made it all the more surprising that I was hired to join the all-male crew at the local 15-minute oil change joint. They were a decidedly down-home and proudly redneck team. The owner—let's call him Carl—was a retired military man who built his career as a mechanic. I will forever be grateful to this late-middle-aged, white, former-military man for giving me a chance in the automotive world. He didn't have to. There was certainly no law preventing him from outright discrimination against me as a queer person. I imagine hiring me caused grumblings among his existing crew. But Carl must have seen something in me—whether it was my eagerness to please or the quirkiness of Phi Beta Kappa college graduate wanting to vacuum cars and check radiator fluid for six bucks an hour, I'm not sure—but he hired me and thus began my multi-year odyssey as a queer woman in the automotive world.

The 15-minute oil change shop was a tough gig. We worked four, 10-hour days a week, with just a 30-minute meal break each day. It was so physically exhausting that I brought bacon sandwiches for lunch just to keep my caloric intake high enough.

But the most difficult part was that, aside from necessary work chatter ("Starting in 3!" "You missed a spot on the windshield!") none of the other workers talked to me. Not a word of social chatter. No one said more than a curt "hi" if I said good morning. It was like I was invisible, ten hours a day. I was miserable, but I was not going to let their treatment of me make me quit.

I was there for probably two months before I had the courage to tell my boss about how I was being ostracized. I asked Carl, "Was there something I did or said that made them not talk to me?"

"You? No. I told them that if they said anything sideways to you, they'd get fired."

Apparently they were afraid to talk to me, for fear of saying something wrong and losing their jobs.

Carl meant well—and he certainly took a bold step to hire dykey-looking me—but in the end it may have been the social pariah status he inadvertently imposed on me that was the hardest part of the job.

## Auto Parts Store, 1995

I learned from that experience. After a several-month stint at the oil-change place, I got a job at the customer service counter at an auto parts store. At this job, I took the initiative to talk to the guys who worked there, having been schooled by a butch friend who taught me how to interact, guy-style. She taught me how to mock-insult them, appreciate their return insults as camaraderie, and talk like "one of the guys." I listened to their stories and gave them advice (and sympathy!) about dating women. I was brash, I was sardonic, and I felt free and fully myself. For many of them, I was the only gay person that they knew and I was reasonably likeable. I like to think I opened the minds of some of these manly men, at least a little bit. I don't miss the crazy hours, the swing shifts, or the low pay, but 30 years later, I still miss how authentic I felt every day walking into work and being 100% myself.

## Self-Employment and Business Networking, 2010s

As I discovered over time, "lesbian" was a not a fully inclusive description of my sexual identity. "Bi" was a closer ("queer" and "rabble-rousing feminist" remain indelible parts of my sense of self). How I came to that conclusion, married a man, settled in big city in the Pacific Northwest—where the wise words of a drag queen and a transwoman help me get in touch with my true Femme self—is a story for another time.

This tale picks up in a gay-friendly big city on the West Coast in the late 2010's. You would think I could have been out as Bi there, but no, for the most part I kept it to myself. Now that I was married to a man, it seemed disrespectful to our relationship to tell people—especially out lesbians—that I was queer. It might sound like I was trolling. So even here, in this rainbow-coated city, for the most part I've kept my sexual identity to myself, and have felt partially shut down for decades because of it.

Probably the oddest business-related experience I've had as a femme, married-to-a-man bisexual woman was at a networking event at a large, local LGBTQ business group. Because of the way I look (high heels, high femme) I felt like I always had to qualify myself: Yes! I am one of you. I've marched, I've been harassed, I've been ostracized. I've been married to a woman and none of my family would attend the wedding. I've been to women's music festivals. I saw k.d. lang live before she was out. I am not an "ally", I am One Of You.

I could have dressed closer to the part (more butch or androgynous), or not mentioned having a husband, but that's not who I am and is no more authentic than staying in the closet. As a result, I came out to some degree in almost every conversation I had at that LGBTQ group, just to clarify who I was and why I was there. It was exhausting—in the one place where I thought I should have been able to be all of myself. In the end, I quit attending their events. Being on the outside looking in, in the one place where I belonged the most, was just too painful.

—Jane D.

CHAPTER SEVEN

# Designing Inclusion

A few things to keep in mind as we go through this section:

- Know the difference between increasing visibility and creating a target.
- You are not creating policy and culture for your queer employees—you are creating it for *all* employees.
- People make bad trade-offs when time or resources are (or are perceived to be) scarce.

## The Big Three

These are my go-to starting points for developing new campaigns or initiatives. I've modified them to better support Inclusion and Diversity (I&D) programs, but the basics are very similar.

Keep in mind, this is not an exhaustive list and much of what's relevant will depend on your unique situation. But I've found that starting with the three larger categories can help surface different themes to consider.

Also, now would be a good time to review the section in Chapter 2 on why initiatives fail. There is a lot of overlap between those elements and the concepts discussed in this section.

Start with insights on the lived experience of the population being served.

- Acknowledge your gaps, educate yourself, and leverage the experts.
- Appreciate the unique challenges and experiences of the population being served, along with the influencing factors. What makes this different?
- Understand and differentiate between orientation, gender identity, expression, and attribution.

Avoid thinking of inclusion as a one-size-fits-all approach.

- Consider the intersectionality and invisibility of this segment.
- Risk, acceptance, stigma, privilege, and access are disproportionate.
- Designing inclusion is extremely nuanced—well-intended, but misinformed, change can result in harm or offense.
- Introduce small, incremental changes within a larger, cohesive strategy.

Be realistic about your organization.

- Perceptions, group dynamics, and potential bias.
- Culture of change or clinging to the status quo?

- How do people receive new information and process change?

- Emerging or mature? Startup or established? Geo-diverse or single location?

- Set the intention. Change doesn't simply occur. This seems evident, but our language usually frames change, such as culture shifts, as occurring almost in a vacuum (for example, war "broke out").

This exercise will help you organize ideas, making sure that the 'right' problem is being addressed, and the "right" solution doesn't introduce unintended consequences.

As you go through each of these elements, revisit the earlier section on building plans, getting clarity on your 'why', etc. Everything in this book eventually connects back.

One constant throughout the design process is reminding people that representation is not a zero-sum equation. Increasing visibility and inclusive language does not erase other identities. The stage is big enough for everyone.

If your organization has been lacking in diversity, breaking out of the homogenous can be interpreted as a kind of erasure to those in the dominant culture.

It's kind of like when two parking spots at the mall are now dedicated to those with certain disabilities or mobility issues. Most people get it and respect the space. Others drive around, shaking their fists at the sky—"Why gods, why? I used to have access to everything. Now I have access to only 98% of everything."

Changes that are interpreted as erasure can trigger a feeling of false competition or potential loss. It taps into the scarcity heuristic, a shortcut our brain takes to attribute value based on availability (real or perceived) and impact to the person if lost.

Except parking lots have finite number of spaces. The inclusion programs you're designing are creating space for everyone. There is room enough for everyone on the stage.

## Avoiding Exclusionary Goals

Remember when I mentioned that even well-intended allies can cause harm or offense? Defining goals for your initiatives includes filtering them for exclusion or unintended consequences.

For example, there has been more focus on issues such as pay equity and improving gender diversity in the tech industry. Companies started announcing bold goals with press releases like Nordstrom's efforts on ensuring pay equity (Nordstrom, 2019).

The promotion starts off as very promising:

> Today, we are pleased to announce we have achieved 100% pay equity for employees of all genders and races.

But then we get to the statement itself:

> We're at nearly 100% pay parity for men and women, which reflects our strong female representation across the company.

We will continue our efforts in this space to build our representation of women at all levels across the organization.

Where did all the other genders from sentence one go? We go from employees of all genders to female representation and women. However unintentionally, this communicates exclusion, that the organization just doesn't get it.

Well-intended, but exclusionary, goals or hugely off-putting missteps are easy to make along the way. Even companies and organizations that promote inclusion for non-binary and gender diverse humans don't always stick the landing on I&D goals.

As part of their continued support of fostering an inclusive and diverse culture, Accenture established its gender diversity goal of "50/50 by 2025." (Accenture, 2019).

Last year, AnitaB.org announced their "Tech Equity for All Women" initiative, stating "We'd like to see 50/50 by 2025." (AnitaB, 2019).

So, does this mean 50% men and 50% women, and too bad for everyone else? Or is it 50% men and 50% everyone else? Messaging like this leads to scarcity, division, and false competition.

As a data geek and business major at heart, I get it. We love to measure and quantify things in business. But, as I said earlier, humans are squishy. Cultivating true inclusion, equity, and access to opportunity starts with being more precise in designing qualitative new ways to evaluate.

Again, it's not a zero-sum equation. Goals like this foster division and exclusion. Representation matters.

I can't emphasize enough the importance of understanding nuances within the population being served by your initiatives.

Customers and employees have to be able to see themselves genuinely reflected in your business. Reflect their words and experiences.

## What to Do When Your Company Gets Called Out

Leading with a defense of what the company (or execs, you, human resources) has *already done* around LGBTQ+ inclusion and diversity is not a good look for anyone.

Inclusion isn't a fixed state. Think of your organization as positioning to level up. It's going to involve a lot of deeper listening and observation, neither of which can happen if you are concentrating on your own response.

Don't make the conversation about you. If your company gets called out on a gap, misstep, unintended consequence (pick your term), own it. If you don't know how to address it, acknowledge that and engage the experts.

People aren't expecting your company to be experts in gender identity and orientation if you sell paint. However, people do expect you to use the resources and expertise needed to cultivate inclusion and representation. To have customers and employees reflected in your brand.

## Policy

*"Acceptance cannot be legislated."*
—Rich Ferraro, COO, GLAAD

True, but legislation absolutely drives acceptance or accelerates its erosion.

Demonstrating a culture of inclusion greatly impacts the degree of acceptance in the community.

Quick reminder before we get started—don't become too hung up on the word "policy." Think of it as a convenient umbrella term for anything from personal guidelines to rules to federal legislation. Yes, these are very different things, but only regarding the scope of influence and your authority to enforce them.

Influence scope: you can have a practice of not watching scary movies after 8 p.m. You cannot extend this as a rule at the city or state level.

Authority to enforce: you can have a personal guideline of driving the speed limit plus 15% more miles per hour. You cannot pull over people who drive more slowly.

So, when I say policy, there are many other potential applications you can consider. The important thing to remember is the far-reaching potential for positive (and negative) influence. It's a splash-and-ripple effect. Drop a rock in the lake and see how far the ripples go. And that's just one superficial dimension.

Policies do a couple of different things. At a basic level, policies give us a framework and floor. These are the rules to which we all agree in order for our continued membership (at work, school, community groups, etc.). This is the primary function that people most associate with policies.

A secondary outcome of policies is how they support or disrupt the social structure. Policies spark conversations and bring different experiences to the forefront. They open a door into one person's perspective, which can lead to a change in understanding.

Take, for example, the introduction of marriage equality in the United States. Decades of legal challenges, voter-based decisions, and legislative bans culminated in the Federal Supreme Court's decision in June 2015. Marriage equality was upheld and bans at the state level were deemed unconstitutional.

But all of that policy making, legislation, and campaigning didn't occur in a vacuum. Emotionally charged topics like this splash and ripple their way through our social structure. Imagine turning on the news and watching a heated discussion over whether you have equal protection under the law. Or, if you even exist. Or if you can be cured? Right, we're back to that again already.

So, fast-forward a couple of years. In 2017, the Journal of American Medical Association published a study showing a decline in suicide attempts among adolescents residing in states with marriage equality (JAMA, 2017). Researchers used data collected by the Centers for Disease Control (CDC) through their Youth Risk Behavior Surveillance System Data, which is comprised of survey responses from a total of 762,678 students across 47 states, collected between 1999-2015.

The results showed a decrease equivalent to 7%, estimating 134,000 fewer suicide attempts among adolescents each year in states with marriage equality. The decrease also persisted for respondents in these states during the two years following policy implementation.

Think about that for a minute. The implications are staggering. LGBTQ+ youth seeing themselves reflected positively, and as having equal legal standing, lessens the rate of suicide attempts.

More specifically, marriage equality provided kids and young adults with examples of their potential for a happy, loving future, if that's what they decide to do. Essentially, these are messages that mitigate risk because they affirm LGBTQ+ people as equal and visible individuals.

If you're stuck on why this is a big deal for queer kiddos, now might be a good time to revisit the discussion in Chapter 3 in the "Why This Is Different" section. As Harvey Milk so famously stated, "You've got to give them hope."

The other side of this influence is seen in the impact of discriminatory policy. Even when these policies don't pass, or are quickly overturned, there is an impact on LGBTQ+ individuals.

When discriminatory policies are proposed, there is a normalization of stigma—discrimination that would be completely unacceptable for any other segment of the population.

This isn't a matter of one ideology over another; discriminatory policy has a splash-and-ripple effect regardless of who implements it.

These policies also spark discussion in the media, community, religious institutions... eventually making it to the workplace. The undertone of discriminatory policy is that while it might be safe to be out now, it might not be so safe in the future.

Remember when we talked about watching strangers argue against your access to bathrooms? Those conversations find their way into homes and communities. They influence early messages that kids receive about what it means to be queer. And when someone's right to equal protection is open for discussion, they become "less than."

The social impact of this also shows up in research. In their 2019 publication of "Accelerating Acceptance," GLAAD found a decrease in social acceptance for the LGBTQ+ community among 18- to 34-year-olds (GLAAD, 2019).

Fewer non-LGBTQ respondents (ages 18-34) identified as allies (45% versus 63% in 2016), and more expressed being uncomfortable learning that a family member is LGBTQ (36% versus 24% in 2016) (GLAAD, 2019).

When we see progress for one segment of the community, it's not uncommon to experience backlash in another segment. That's how people in power keep marginalized populations in check—they keep them in opposite corners.

### Disrupt the Industry—C'mon, It'll Be Fun!

As of this writing, multiple states provide an alternative marker, other than female or male, on drivers' licenses and identification cards. It started with Washington DC, then Oregon, then California... culminating in now 17 states (plus DC) adopting this decision.

So, then what happened? The opportunity to disrupt the industry and demonstrate inclusion.

In early 2019, several major airlines announced plans to provide gender non-specific indicators for passengers when making reservations. Meaning that people with an "X" indicator on their state-issued license didn't have to contort into an "F" or "M" check box when booking a trip. And their flight information matched the state-issued identification presented at the airport, because both have a gender non-specific marker.

It's important to make a distinction here... I tend to use the term *gender non-specific* rather than *gender neutral* because it feels more precise to me. There is not a gender being specified when a person can select "X".

Occasionally you might hear alternative markers or indicators (such as "X") referred to as *non-binary* options, which for whatever reason causes confusion at times.

Stick with me for a minute—or feel free to read ahead if you already get where I'm going.

Including gender non-specific indicators, like using an "X" or "prefer not to disclose" instead of only "female" or "male" can be referred to as *non-binary* options because they are not limiting someone to a binary, either/or tick box on a form, license, application, etc.

This is where it can seem confusing at first. Sometimes non-binary can appear to be the only alternative for humans who identify other than female or male. But gender identity is a broad array. When we talk about gender diversity outside of a female/male binary, this includes identities such as gender-fluid, agender, non-binary, and so on.

Again, we are trying to condense a complex and uniquely human experience into words. Language itself presents a limitation.

And you are not expected to become an expert in gender identity. Just understand there are different ways of being and others may or may not feel like sharing their personal info with you. Now, I'm way off topic, but it felt like an important side road away from Labeltown.

Where was I? Airlines, right.

Two trade associations, the International Air Transport Association and Airlines for America, approved the use of gender non-specific indicators for passengers during the reservation process. Delta, American Airlines, United, and Southwest announced similar programs were in the works. Air Italy was the first airline in the EU to make the switch, with other European airlines exploring the idea.

Less than 18 months after states introduced gender non-specific markers, airlines modified their systems, processes, and policies to make this feature available to customers.

That's no small task. Consider the amount of time, focus, and resources needed to implement that much change. Not to mention the additional training, education, and support necessary at that scale.

Along the way, these companies also signaled a profound message to their consumer base. *We see you. We value you. We recognize your humanity and you are welcome here.* Changes like these are sending a powerful ripple effect out into society. They used their position and took a stand.

"Every customer. Every flight. Every day."

That's no small message.

United launched their new program using the tag line "Fly as you identify." Announcements on social media were met with a blend of celebration and snark, topped with a smattering of "How *could* you?!" pearl-clutching backlash. Such as...

> I am not flying any airline that is too stupid to know men from women.
> Do you think this delusion will win you customers? You thought this was a good business decision to endorse this nonsense?
> I believe in science. There are only two genders. I wish businesses would just run their business and stop shoving this stuff down our throat.
> OMG, that's a real thing??? I thought it was a joke. What a screwed-up country this is turning into.

Oh, Internet comment sections, you never disappoint.

When I talk to clients about this example, they usually have lots of excellent questions. Most center around implementation. They focus on the mechanics and heavy lifting involved with such a change. Sometimes they ask about managing the eventual backlash from a segment of the population that might not agree.

We discuss all of that: things to consider, what to expect, when to call in specialists. And the real work starts: partnership with experts; continued focus; deep understanding of all the business components impacted; taking a stand; being equipped to support and engage effectively when customers show up at the door.

One of the reasons these implementations went so well across the four airlines is because they brought in experts. The Human Rights Campaign and the Trevor Project were involved in partnership.

Because introducing this change (policy, process, new way of doing things) has the potential for far-reaching social impact, you need to be able to back it up. By "you" I mean you, your organization, your employees, your infrastructure, your call centers... all of it needs to be equipped to follow through. Inclusion lives in the daily experience.

Now, if I could just get Delta to stop saying, "ladies and gentlemen" at the beginning of each announcement. Come on, we can do better. Passengers? Peeps? Flotation device adjacent humans? So many options here.

NARRATIVE

# The Kids Are Alright

I am a teacher. I had never given much thought to gender or young students being LGTBQ. I assumed that was something that raised its head in older teenagers and adults. I addressed my students as "boys and girls" or "ladies and gentlemen" without a thought. I had boys line up here, and girls line up here.

My thinking on this has evolved over the past 10 years of teaching and I try to address my students in a gender-neutral way, "friends" or "students" instead of "boys and girls," lining up by other attributes instead of gender. I have several students to thank for helping my understanding evolve.

One day, I was working on an art project with a class of kindergarteners who were studying fairy tales. The students could make themselves a king or queen, prince or princess, in our story. One little boy asked if he could have the princess template for the project. I gave him the princess template and he told me he had a princess living inside his head and that when he was grown up, she would be able to come out and play. He asked me not to say anything to his parents because when he said it at home it made his mom cry and his dad get mad.

For many years after he left my classroom, he would come in before school and "change". The changes were subtle:

a different shirt that a friend would provide, a set of fake tattoo sleeve gloves would be turned inside out to become elegant evening gloves, hair would be styled a bit different. I have watched this student grow over the years, and never waver in their sense of inner self.

My interactions with this student prompted me to seek out more information about gender diversity, and how it appears in young students. Since then, I have had three other elementary students who have shared with me that they are transgender or non-binary. I am always so honored that they trust me enough to share. I am also amazed at their strength, bravery, and sense of self. I am lucky to work in a school district that recognizes them, allows them to be themselves, and supports them.

When we had our first student transition, they did so by un-enrolling, then re-enrolling with their new name and gender. Our district provided training to staff and to the students in their grade level to better understand the idea of gender. It was so helpful, both for those who knew a small bit about LGBTQ and those who knew nothing. Just like gender is a spectrum, knowledge of it is also a spectrum.

While I have had four students who have shared their gender journey with me, I am sure there are others who have not. I think it is important to remember that anyone you meet may be LGBTQ, even if they are not publicly out, and it is so important to create an environment where they feel safe and respected. Learning is a lifelong journey and I know I am still learning about how to better create an environment my students can feel accepted all the time.

—Lifelong Learner

CHAPTER EIGHT

# Implementation Doesn't Have to Be Scary

Think of this chapter as combining the nuance of LGBTQ+ inclusion with the basic mechanics necessary to successfully launch effective projects.

Some of the content will apply to launching projects overall. Some will overlap across designing I&D initiatives for multiple underrepresented populations.

Again, don't let the word "projects" throw you off.

Think of it the same way as the word "policy" in the earlier section. It's a convenient umbrella term to describe any initiative that involves an element of planning, requires buy-in from other stakeholders, impacts people other than yourself, has some element of working across teams or individuals, etc.

Organizing a movie night for you and five friends has the elements of a project, as does launching a product in multiple countries. It's a matter of scale, impact, and the potential for catastrophic career-ending outcomes. No pressure. It's probably fine.

Projects also follow a similar cycle: define the problem being solved, propose and develop a solution, implement, and observe the outcome or results. At the end of the day, this is largely about overcoming obstacles. And those obstacles are not always going to be grounded in the reasons given.

Also, take time out during this process to evaluate change fatigue. This can show up as introducing your changes too quickly (saturation time, measure effectiveness, controlled environment) and too many changes coming from other channels (changes to internal systems, reorganizations, seasonal or cyclical upticks for business units, etc.).

Now is when the timelines and plans you created earlier really start to come in handy. Engage with stakeholders and impacted teams to make sure everyone is aligned.

Change fatigue can also show up as frustration. Progress is not happening fast enough for some and is too much, too fast for others. Go back to the long-term strategy you outlined. Sharing information and transparency goes a long way to smoothing out the curve of change.

## Understand the System

Implementation is where you'll begin to discover many of the factors that weren't considered or fully understood.

Try not to beat yourself up too much—this is a learning process. Each launch is going to inform the next project. It's like testing for leaks in a pipe. You want to control the flow and watch for signs of what was missed or too small to see.

This means getting an end-to-end operational understanding of the process, system, teams, and procedures—whatever it is that you use to introduce change.

My favorite example is the regulation introduced to limit how much liquid each passenger could carry onto a commercial flight.

Days after this change was first in effect, airlines were overwhelmed by the dramatic uptick in checked bags. The limit didn't prevent people from bringing larger amounts of liquids, it just made them put it into a checked bag. Somewhere in the decision chain this seemingly obvious scenario was missed.

Now take a step back and add more diversity in perspectives. Imagine that same 'policy to implementation' discussion was a series of conversations to explore potential outcomes. And not just leadership or policy influencers. The end-to-end impact of this new regulation would need to be understood from multiple angles.

But from an operational perspective, things start to become complicated. Impacted channels could include gate agents, baggage handlers, flight attendants, representatives from large and small airports, domestic and international providers, ground crews, communications teams, etc.

You see how quickly this can seem unwieldy—it becomes a chaotic, time-consuming exercise that requires a great deal of negotiating skills and finesse. The trade-off is developing a deep enough understanding of the system, without getting so far into the weeds that you become stuck.

This is where we're going to tie a few previous sections together. For example, going back to the sections on why I&D initiatives fail, many of these areas are related to lack of dedicated resources and expertise.

But let's take it further. Understanding the nuances of gender identity and orientation helps guide the policy discussion. Being able to manage people through change leads to more effective implementation. Creating clear goals and problem statements provides a framework that others can support and rally around. Defining meaningful evaluation points allows for course correction and informs future initiatives.

It all fits together.

## Bracketing and Reflexivity

Saving this for the implementation section was intentional. It's important to learn the mechanics of navigating change first, and then how to manage all the wonderful new unconscious bias that comes along with that knowledge.

Imagine if Glinda the Good Witch told Dorothy about the power of those ruby slippers in the first five minutes instead of sending her down the Yellow Brick Road to find the Wizard? Shortest movie ever, and *Of Mice and Men* walks away with the Oscar for Best Original Music Score instead.

It's part of the journey. Starting with the end in mind includes holding back what you already know. Stick with me here.

Bracketing and reflexivity are concepts related to qualitative research. "Reflexivity" is a fancy term to describe that the researcher is part of the system being observed; subject to the same preconceptions and bias interpretations as everyone else.

One method to acknowledge the researcher as being a mere mortal and (hopefully) mitigate personal bias when collecting, analyzing, and synthesizing data is through "bracketing." Again, do as the kids say and "check yourself before you wreck yourself." Am I using that right?

Essentially, bracketing is an exercise that involves documenting your preconceived ideas, experiences, potential blind spots, and other beliefs or knowledge that could shape data interpretation.

Taking time to bracket these assumptions, or any speculation about what will be learned, gets you to more clearly defined goals, intentions, and problem statements.

Let's go back to the example of airlines and unintended bottlenecks. If I was looking at lines and long wait times getting through security, most of my bias would be from personal travel experiences. Lines back up because people are unfamiliar with the process, are helping children in tow, etc. My suggestions to improve the lines might include a "families" lane and an express lane for frequent flyers (assuming generalities that translate into throughput).

However, observing these lines from the perspective of security experts, the delays could be perceived not as "problems," but necessary for adequate screening.

An agent who is responsible for fielding calls from unhappy customers would have entirely different thoughts on potential causes and solutions.

Brackets for each of these individuals would reflect different preconceptions, blind spots, and biases. Comparing these lists during a collaborative planning session would more accurately inform the problem statement and project intention.

Start with outlining why you believe something is a problem and any existing thoughts on the situation. It doesn't have to be a perfect or exhaustive depiction. This is a starting point that can (and should) be refined throughout the project.

### Working Across Teams

Unfortunately, at work we're usually so intent on accomplishing the next thing that focus and planning can feel like a waste of time. How often have you heard managers resist planning sessions because they "don't have time"? Investing an intentional act breaks the momentum we've convinced ourselves is a sign of success. People are attracted to making bad decisions as quickly and effectively as possible.

Have you ever watched a homogeneous group of cooperative people reach decisions? It's fantastic. Super-efficient. There is nothing like it. Go into a 45-minute meeting, listen to the proposal, politely challenge the default team leader, walk it back, demonstrate agreeable behavior to keep the peace, and support the flawed proposal.

Even more interesting is what happens next.

Over the following 'x' number of months, each of these team members will continue down the agreed-to path, even when confronted with increasing evidence of bad direction. There is also a great deal of intellectual gymnastics going on with you in the background to reaffirm that going along with the default leader was the right decision.

Eventually things become so bad that the team will vehemently reject conflicting information, diminishing any diversity of thought and further digging in on the project's direction.

Sound familiar?

The extent to which your brain works to protect the ego is admirable. Cognitive theories aside, people are more rationalizing than rational.

We're all susceptible to it. The more time, resources, and personal ego (or sense of self) invested in a decision, the less likely people are to admit an error and course correct. Cognitive bias and scarcity of time makes for bad decisions; along with an inability to acknowledge and course correct.

Ever watched a team challenge each other? Present data from different aspects of the project, build on each other's ideas until a series of optimal strategies are reached? The same elements that contribute to these teams also support inclusion. We'll discuss what's missing in later chapters.

Building a cohesive and high-performing team starts with establishing a safe environment for taking risks or trying new strategies.

The same is true for cultivating inclusion; people must feel valued and recognized as themselves. Each unique aspect of an individual contributes new perspective and approaches to solving problems.

People can't do that if they feel unsafe or need to mute themselves. Bringing an individual's whole, authentic self to the organization requires courage. Developing an enthusiastically inclusive workplace... that takes leadership.

### Avoiding Dumpster Fires

Everything was great, right up until the point it wasn't. Then, everything was very, very wrong.

One critical aspect of implementation is to develop an intuition for when things are going wrong. Maybe not even to the point of going wrong; more like being 'off.' Like a corporate version of Spidey sense. As you become more involved with projects, embrace this sixth sense—or at least pay attention to it.

'Something off' can show up as an unusually tense meeting, vague updates on status, or a carefully worded email. Alone these could all be chalked up to a team member having a bad day. But watch when they all start occurring together or appearing shortly after another event.

This is when you dust off those contingency plans from that earlier section and start off-loading all the new things that can go wrong.

Imagine ideas to be passengers getting off a plane. You're patiently waiting at the gate and all you can see is the few ideas emerging from first class. Those elite status concerns are blocking your view of all the other ideas queued up behind them in your brain.

Off-loading possible events that could derail your project does a couple of things. First, it will help you visualize them in a way that could spark other realizations. There may be gaps in your plan that come to light only in the midst of all these Post-it notes.

Think about those meetings where one person takes up all the oxygen. Monopolizes the conversation. Brings everything back to themself. Yes, super annoying.

Beyond that, it also limits the expression of other ideas, viewpoints, and considerations. That one concern currently dominating your attention prevents you from seeing other things. Writing out each potential issue gives you clarity. From there, you can start attributing an actual value based on all the other factors.

Side benefit of this process? Nothing is lost. Even issues that go beyond the back-burner types. Maybe a few are such low priority that they actually fall off a back burner and become a tiny, crisp bit on the foil. You can keep everything and refer back as things evolve. When an obstacle thwarts progress, check back on these items and see if one might be worth another review.

Secondly, once they are out you can start to think about them less abstractly. Potential blockers can be prioritized based on likelihood and impact. None of this is new from a project management perspective, but it's critical to have things organized based on reality.

Too many amazing projects never see the light of day because magical thinking takes over. The desire to launch takes over and people ignore warning signs that something needs course correction.

A zombie apocalypse might be considered unlikely, so you categorize this with other "Devastating, but unlikely" scenarios like a pandemic or massive snowstorm.

Have a plan of things to monitor and how to respond. It doesn't have to be perfect or exhaustive; this is a starting point from which you can build as the project (and the number of knowns) develops.

Next category, "Possible, with various impacts." This area will depend on your industry and organizational type (go back to the Chapter 8 section, "Be Realistic About Your Organization").

Last, group together anything that feels "Likely, with various impacts" or "Less likely, but this would be the end of us." This analysis comes last because you are going to spend more time here. These situations tend to need closer monitoring and can sneak up on you. Things like change resisters gaining sway, sudden loss of resourcing, or a shift in organizational priorities.

Problems in this category are also more likely to dog-pile or intersect, making smaller challenges into devastating project enders.

A good example of this is the slow creep of resistance to change. It's easy to get behind change until about six weeks in;

that's when the effort starts to outpace the excitement and novelty of culture shift. Think back to those January goals—about February or early March things stagnate.

Imagine a situation in which change resisters drag and chip away at the momentum. Then a seemingly unrelated "Likely, with various impact" crack appears. Something like a shift in organizational priorities or reduction in approved overtime.

If you're not plugged in and visibly advocating the benefits of an initiative, it's likely to be cut. Maybe not canceled altogether... just "postponed" for right now. You know, "Until this crisis passes. Then we can pick it back up. Because, remember, inclusion is important to the organization. We need everyone to be a team player and help out."

Sound familiar? And this isn't unique to I&D projects. However, they are often perceived to be less critical in the grand scheme of things. Be ready and keep your focus on the larger plan. Remember: incremental changes with a cohesive strategy.

### Communicating the Change

As with any organizational change, communicating something new is a big factor in a successful launch. The message itself is important—people want to know what to expect, how they might be impacted, and (let's be honest here) what's in it for them.

But there is more to receiving a message than reading the words. Example, people give different levels of attention to an email from the CEO than from accounting. No shade to accounting and finance teams, it's just the reality of how humans filter. CEO email could mean a major announcement; accounting is more likely a dry reminder to send in a form.

Deciding how to announce initiatives around LGBTQ+ inclusion should happen early in the process. If the change involves new options from a drop-down menu on HR portal, should the announcement come from the CEO? Or HR? Or the I&D executive? It depends.

There are multiple factors in deciding the ideal communication channel. Which is why you're going to highlight this during implementation and build it into the schedule. See how easy?

Things to consider:

- How are updates or announcements typically managed?
- What is the right level of leadership or executive support for this?
- What is the magnitude of the change? Is it better supported through a less formal channel?

One last item: avoid framing the communication as only being for, or benefiting, the LGBTQ+ population (unless for some reason it actually does only impact this segment). Inclusive programs and policies benefit all employees.

NARRATIVE

# Dichotomous: Two Very Different Environments

My name is Kai and I identify as an openly queer and androgynous individual. Despite my masculine-leaning exterior, I use she/her pronouns. Over the course of 20 years, I have had the privilege of working as an administrator in various industries and companies of different sizes.

Between 2005 and 2008 I was employed with the third largest telecom company, better known as Cox Communications. My experience at this company was unforgettable. Cox was at the prime of its business and had just won the top awards presented by JD Powers. I worked as an independent contractor for almost a year, until I was offered a full-time position. Both the culture and the benefits package were attractive. From the first day of full-time employment, I was accruing PTO hours. By the end of the first month, I had already earned about two days of vacation.

In addition to the PTO hours, any employee could purchase a computer on the company's credit through payroll deductions. This proved to be a viable option for someone who did not wish to incur debt on her credit card. I was able to secure a laptop for my secondary collegiate endeavors and potential future side business.

Health coverage was amazing as well. The annual deductions were so low that it was easy to meet the requirements. Before same sex marriage was legalized, this company was already offering coverage for domestic partnerships.

Furthermore, the company believed in diversity so much that a diversity council was established and I was selected to help represent my Network Development department. Two of my colleagues were openly gay as well. I also felt comfortable with the diversity of the leadership. One of the managers was an openly gay woman.

Cox also believed in education and career advancement. We were encouraged to attend Cox's own university. I could attend these classes on company time to develop or enhance certain skill sets. Financial assistance was available for those who desired to complete their undergraduate education [with an outside university] and I would have taken advantage of such opportunity if I'd been employed with Cox three years prior.

The open-door policy of Cox was outstanding. If I didn't feel comfortable addressing a particular issue with my current supervisor, I knew I could safely speak with another. Even the HR department was swift in its resolution efforts when I encountered an issue with a fellow employee's conduct towards me. Whenever the core leadership of my department met weekly, the leaders opened a portion of their meetings and invited various employees to discuss any suggestions that we had to improve the department.

In terms of the operations, the tech tools that Cox utilized were advanced for its time as well. I was first exposed to the incredible software of two of the largest tech giants: Oracle and Salesforce.

By contrast, the current company I have been working for almost a decade at, could use an overhaul in the diversity and inclusion department. Although the line-up of executives and top management featured in this three-generational NYC company's website appear to reflect diversity and inclusion, there are not enough Asians in upper management. Within two years of my employment, my CFO and mentor promoted me to become the divisional director of administration for my department. My largest contribution to my company was spearheading the efforts to streamline our work order tracking capabilities by collaborating with a computer programmer.

Together, we produced a proprietary sequel database. A lot of the business practices from this company were archaic. The company only realized the potential of tech tools like Salesforce a couple of years ago.

At this company, the benefit package is okay, but not incredible. When I inquired about the health coverage for my partner of almost 15 years, my HR department manager's response was somewhat discouraging, revolving around the term "civil union". This translated to me as "getting married at city hall." It was sad and tragic to hear that this was the best this company had to offer in terms of diversity and inclusion. There are no Employee Resource Groups at this company of almost 500 employees, between several offices spanning in three states. Only one Latina woman represents the entire HR department. As a result, I am in the closet at work. Maybe two women know about my queer identity and have treated me no differently.

I feel like I have hit the ceiling at work, in terms of advancing up the organizational ladder. The highest position that I could attain is Chief Administrative Officer, which is currently held by a white woman.

Despite my position, I have struggled with the lack of empowerment for three years. When I realized that the changes I tried to enact were not taken seriously, I decided to search for opportunities outside employment to empower myself. I was impacted and inspired by Leanne Pittsford and the amazing global tech organization she founded, known as Lesbians Who Tech & Allies. Eventually, I taught myself how to code using online courses. In the future, I aspire to launch one the first Asian queer tech consulting firms in my city. It feels important to see both of my identities reflected there.

CHAPTER NINE

## Inclusion as a Daily Practice

Getting your organization from "we have a policy" to a culture of inclusion starts with meeting people where they are, not where you live. Let's flip the script here for a minute and look at opportunities where your organization can get better at inclusion (*Inclusive AF!*).

Inclusion, like any other cultural value, doesn't just happen—it's an intentional daily practice.

**First, to Recap:**

- Inclusion lives in the daily experience of employees, clients, and consumers.

- Valuing people as individuals—each with their own unique story and perspective—always starts with visibility.

- Inclusion is grounded in a very human need; we all want to be seen as ourselves, as who we really are.

- It's the other side of authenticity; there is tremendous value in connecting with people as "I see you."

- Keep this list handy—it's great info to motivate resource holders to sign a check and support your initiatives.

Again, the challenge is that to get these results, a couple of things also need to be present. Teams must operate in a safe, trusting environment.

This doesn't mean only happy fun times, free of all conflict. Frustration can be a necessary part of change. That is where the growth happens. Healthy levels of challenging ideas and talking through different perspectives are part of the journey.

Safe and trusted means that people are valued and accepted as themselves. All the energy goes into solving the business problem at hand, rather than navigating politics or conforming to the group for protection.

Much of the reason that company cultures struggle with lasting change rests in our need to remain comfortable. Not necessarily cozy "comfortable," like sitting on a posh recliner, but "comfortable" in having a sense of familiarity and predictability.

People need to learn the daily practice of inclusion. It's like having a manual for running the power saw, but not providing consistent guidance on how to avoid losing digits (yours or others).

Repeat after me, Inclusion is not:

- Having a policy (even binders full of really good ones).
- Like a flu shot (something you think about once a year, if you have time).
- A project you implement.
- Possible without a culture that internalizes and sustains it.

## The Power of Language

The words you use and hear shape the way you think and perceive. They have significant influence over that unconscious bias filtering and prioritizing the information in your head.

Let's go back to the section in Chapter 4 on how your brain is lazy. Selecting words to express ourselves follows a similar process. We tend to continually use terms that worked for us in the eighth grade. Sure, our vocabulary has likely expanded since then, but in the pursuit of expediency it's easier to stick with default words. Not much thought goes into it.

One of the least expensive and easier to implement forms of inclusion involves changing our day-to-day language. It starts with taking a step back and unlearning.

Our culture puts gender everywhere. Gender is assigned to toys, clothes, sports, acceptable behaviors, aptitudes, and so much more.

In English, gender shows up in words we use to describe humans. For example, terms that use "man" as a placeholder for "person"—such as "man-hours" or "manpower" to describe estimates of human effort, any "[occupation]-man," and using "he" or "him" to describe a generic person in a hypothetical situation.

These examples are usually the point at which at least one person in the audience will start rolling their eyes. Stick with me.

Words and phrases like "fireman," "man-hours," and "all men are created equal" erase the possibilities for other gender identities. Before someone starts muttering about 'political correctness', let's review everything we've learned in earlier sections.

Representation matters. Visibility matters. Your employees have to be able to see themselves reflected in your company and brand.

Even our understanding of showing respect. Should we address others as Sir and Ma'am, Mr. or Mrs., or Miss or Ms.? Mx.? Each of these is an opportunity to provide a respectful greeting, or unintentionally misgender and alienate an entire segment of the population. And the challenge is that, unless they tell you, odds are not in your favor to get this right.

Use this knowledge to create more robust greetings, like "Good morning, all of you amazing humans!" Embrace using 'they' to describe a person in your examples. For example, "When a customer comes in, they typically go to the popcorn counter first." Practice being intentional with your words.

### Who's Down with OPP? (Other People's Pronouns)

Let's go back to what grandma said about not eating right before swimming. If you spent your entire life waiting 31 minutes between food and the pool, being asked to swim on a full stomach would feel wrong. Depending on how much you were protected by adhering to this guideline, it might trigger some anxiety or discomfort to even watch someone else swim right after eating.

That's OK, lean into it. Give those "grammatical correctness" feelings a big ol' hug and then send them on their way.

Because "they" as a singular, gender non-specific pronoun… that's a thing. It has a long historical legacy, has been accepted by the APA in writing guidelines, and was Merriam-Webster's Word Of The Year in 2019. This is happening, and you will be fine.

As people move away from the concept of gender as binary, using pronouns other than "her" or "him" is becoming increasingly more common. Defining the words that describe you is a powerful way to reclaim this very personal, innate sense of self.

Using they/them pronouns (or ze/zir, or sie/hir) instead of she/her or he/him gives voice to express one's own sense of self. Our collective obligation in this is to respect and recognize the humanity of individuals.

Rather than assuming what pronouns a new employee or colleague uses, create space for them to tell you, without putting the onus on them to bring it up. Then remember to use the pronouns they've indicated. Practice, out loud when possible.

Also, keep in mind that our understanding and vocabulary are both evolving rapidly. Don't focus on memorizing every possible pronoun that can be used. This is about understanding there are different ways of being and avoiding assumptions.

Even if you don't fully understand it, honoring pronouns is absolutely necessary. This is not up for negotiation—it's about recognizing the humanity in another person.

Here are a few last things to think about:

- Pronouns are for everyone and everyone has pronouns. Share the responsibility of inclusion and don't leave the burden to one segment of employees. Recognize that not everyone uses "she" or "he" pronouns.

- Create social norms around pronouns. Model behavior by including your pronouns in an email signature block, or with your bio and introductions. (My name is Jen. I use 'she/her' pronouns; My name is Jen, pronouns are 'she/her.')

## Policy Does Not Equal Practice

Inclusion isn't policy—it's the experience in which humans operate.

Think of it as a model home: policy is the code that ensures no lead paint is used, and daily practice is the machine that makes it smell like you've just baked cookies. Or that part of the oven where you can warm rolls until everything else is done. OK, probably not exactly like that, but c'mon, that oven feature is pretty awesome.

We organize ourselves between written frameworks (policy) and unwritten modeled behaviors (social norms). Policy is necessary as the floor. Intentional daily practices that contribute to inclusion at the individual level—that's what lifts people up.

Toxic or exclusionary behavior does not need to reach the level of abuse before it negatively impacts everyone who is exposed. And offensive questions and behaviors that come from a well-intended or uninformed place still suck. They contribute to a soul-crushing existence at work.

Last, please keep in mind that it's not the responsibility of LGBTQ+ people to educate you or share their experiences. It's their prerogative, for sure, but not their job. It's exhausting. They are also not the 'representative slice of bacon' for an entire segment of the population.

It's a culture shift. A culture *change*—that's an action word right there. It's not a culture that "occurred" or "woke up like this." Action words. And they call for intentional focus in order to develop into a daily practice: your new social norm.

## Employees, Yes, but Look for Other Areas to Improve:

- Building new rewards programs for customers.
- Guest relations teams and support centers.
- Customer satisfaction and promotional surveys.
- Online reservations and scheduling apps.

CHAPTER TEN

# Let's Wrap Things Up and Get to Work

Congratulations on making it through! So, now what? You have new perspectives and strategies—what happens next?

Before the momentum wanes, or you become overwhelmed with where to begin, take a few minutes to review.

Much of the impact and way forward will be determined by your current reality. Industry, size of organization, access to funding or resources, receptiveness to change—each will influence how and where you start.

My go-to approach at this phase is defining a "crawl, walk, run" plan. The beauty of going through this exercise is that it highlights what you can do immediately(-ish) and with zero budget, building up to a longer-term map of systemic, well-funded, change.

Gather up those ideas you captured on Post-it notes earlier. (See? I told you those would come in handy.) Find a white board, empty wall space—whatever—and start organizing the ideas by similarity, overlap, and themes. Some people put them into circles; I prefer columns, it doesn't matter. The intention is to separate ideas into distinct groups (for now).

This exercise can feel like when you stare at one of those 3-D pictures at the mall. The trick is to rest your eyes and stare, unblinking, until a giraffe magically appears amidst the color patterns.

Organizing Post-its into themes feels odd at first. Maybe a few go together; most fall into a miscellaneous category. Keep looking, and patterns will emerge. Ideas will start to connect in ways you hadn't considered. New ones pop up. Your vision begins to take shape.

Or, it doesn't. In which case you take a step back and let things percolate for a minute. Look at how the idea is described: does it still make sense to you? Don't overthink it, this is at the Post-it note stage. "More options for informal mentoring" can be one that connects to "Increase visibility of our Employee Resource Group." And both of these can connect to "Get a seat at an upcoming recruiting event."

Get creative. Be ambitious. Think bigger. This is all part of the process. Eventually, you will see the giraffe.

## Crawl, Walk, and Run Projects

From here, you are ready to start organizing the ideas into stages: crawl, walk, run. Pick your own verb or series of words. One client became enamored with "Ready, Steady, GO" and then there was no stopping them.

The point of crawl, walk, run is to show you what can be accomplished across a range of limited resources and time, moving up to longer-term initiatives with larger impact.

To keep momentum, I suggest landing on two or three solid crawl projects that you can realistically complete within the next 45 days. You! All by yourself—with no budget. Think of this as a test drive of the process.

**Crawl** projects look like this:

- Actions can be completed in the next 30–45 days.
- They build a foundation for larger projects.
- Little to no funding is needed.
- Actions can be completed in addition to your other priorities.

The "Crawl" stage includes activities like adding your pronouns to an email auto signature, updating standard company forms to include "Mx." (pronounced 'mix') as a gender non-specific honorific, or using "they/them" pronouns when gender is immaterial. ("The delivery driver left their notebook behind," or "They left a guest pass for me at the front desk.")

Crawl projects should also land squarely within your authority or realm of control. Other departments might be interested in partnering, but this is not the stage to hand out edicts if there are change resisters. You, and your amazing inclusion initiatives, are in a building phase. Think of these as "fail fast and learn" testing cycles.

Your next projects will be informed by everything that was learned during these cycles, factoring for any other changes in the environment.

**Walk** projects are a little more involved.

- Actions can be completed in two to six months.
- They focus on expansion and growth.
- Projects are possibly dependent on the completion of Crawl projects, or need more time due to complexity.

The "Walk" stage starts to involve a wider scope of influence and more impactful change.

- Ask potential vendors/suppliers about their Inclusion and Diversity practices.
- Create inclusive group norms (for example, challenge each other to stop saying "guys" when addressing non-male-identified humans).
- Review policy, surveys, intake forms, and related materials for bias, or gender in language where it isn't necessary.

**Run** projects are still in ideation at this point.

- These are longer-term forecasting and visioning initiatives.
- Planning and implementation may not start for 12–18+ months.
- Initiatives likely require larger investments of time, allocation of resources, and support at the executive or leadership level.

You will probably not have enough data or soak time (rate at which people absorb "new") to start here. Get a few crawl and walk projects out in the world first.

"Run" projects have the potential for a larger organizational culture shift.

We covered a great example of a run earlier, with Delta and other airlines introducing the option of using gender non-specific pronouns during the booking process. That decision created a new standard across the industry; requiring significant investment of time and resources to accommodate all the related changes. The success of this was largely related to the degree of support across these companies, and a strategic partnership with an external organization of experts (in this case, The Trevor Project).

"Run" projects have incredible potential for impact outside the organization. They also carry substantial risk of harm or damage if executed without adequate thought, research, and exploration of unintended consequences. This is a really good time to leverage experts outside your organization.

As you begin to organize your thoughts into projects, view these categories as building blocks. Remember, lasting change is not a linear process. If something isn't working, or feels forced, take a step back and revaluate.

And, yes, you can.

NARRATIVE

# Bruce (West Hollywood, 1985)

Bruce was my friend. More specifically, he was the first friend I made after moving to LA. We worked together in a crappy budget store on Hollywood Boulevard.

Bruce was gay—like, super gay—and his tendency toward drama was only enhanced by his accent. Growing up in a small Georgia town was less than awesome, so he showed up in LAX one day with two suitcases and no job.

We'd typically get stuck doing inventory. This consisted of three or four of us sitting on the floor counting giant bras or potted plants or whatever our boss was convinced needed counting. At this point you need to imagine four individuals with questionable judgment and an as yet undeveloped sense of decorum.

Eventually we'd escalate our ridiculousness to a point beyond Bruce's capacity "to even" (as the kids say these days).

This tipping point would be highlighted by Bruce shouting (in his super-gay, super-Southern style), "Y'all need Jesus!" Then he'd throw down giant bra number whatever and stomp off to the front register.

That's where he kept the weed. It was the mid 1980s, stop judging.

Bruce was my friend. More than anything he wanted to be loved. A long-term relationship, complete with a white picket fence and slow talking on the front porch swing: this was his vision for the future.

Finding love in LA is not so easy; even less so for a queer ginger in 1985. He lived with his boyfriend, a caterer and SoCal native. Good, not great, was how Bruce described their six-month relationship. It ended horribly, not long before I was scheduled to return home to Seattle.

Bruce had lost weight, but that's not really surprising considering the post-break-up grief and stress. He found a new place and bought a three-foot statue of Michelangelo's David to commemorate starting over. Things seemed to be moving along.

After I returned to Seattle, Bruce and I stayed in touch, mostly through letters. Actual handwritten letters—I know!

He wrote to me about our crappy store, the homeless street performers, and his occasional forays into the dating world. A few months went by without an update and I started moving along in my own Seattle life.

Finally, a letter arrived with Bruce's familiar swoopy cursive writing. But it was postmarked from Georgia. The message itself didn't make a lot of sense—he had to move back home, something about health issues. I couldn't imagine a situation in LA that would be so bad to make moving back in with your parents seem like a better option. But he had done exactly that.

Moved back to the small town that treated him, in his words, like a freak. More than 30 years later I can still hear the pain in his voice and see the tears in his eyes when he said that word... "freak."

"They treated me like I was some kind of freak... something from a sideshow walking around their neighborhood."

I wrote him back and sent along some postcards from the city. Seattle is beautiful and blue. I thought the juxtaposition might give him hope. Or at least a full-on eye-roll from the worst pun ever: "You otter see Seattle!"

Being from the south, Bruce was equipped with a seemingly endless supply of odd phrases. My all-time favorite was "Like a honeybee in the hive just a-buzzin'!" This was used to describe someone (usually me at the time) who was strangely productive.

His next letter was even more disjointed. It made no sense and sometimes his normally carefully crafted sentences drifted off into nothing. The only recognizable piece of Bruce in that letter was a tiny drawing of a bee on the envelope. He never wrote me again. My letters and subsequent postcards came back stamped "Return to sender."

No one from our circle of friends knows exactly what happened. My fear is that he contracted HIV and became too ill to continue in LA. It's a hard city without a support network. The thought of this amazing, kind, funny human spending his last days with 'family' who were incapable of accepting him is painful. He deserved better. He deserved his picket fence and porch swing; he should have enjoyed some slow talking while sitting next to the love of his life.

He deserved to see marriage equality become a reality. To chase sunrises. To get old and fat. (No, seriously, he was very much looking forward to both those things.)

# CHAPTER ELEVEN

## Until We Meet Again …

Now that we've gotten to know each other a little better, why not keep in touch? Our world is at a turning point and anyone who discounts the potential for one person to affect change hasn't been paying attention. This is about more than you or I shaping a single outcome; our conversations can adjust perceptions across every ecosystem to which we come in contact.

A colleague jokingly shared that 2020 is unfolding as if a time traveler kept coming back to 'fix' something, each attempt resulting in even more dire results. I can't disagree. Three months into the year millions of people lost their jobs; many others were still working but counting the days since they last had to wear pants; Las Vegas closed. Closed. Las Vegas. Closed.

As humans, we can only process so much before short-term memory integration is impacted. It's a coping mechanism. Events that were shocking only a few months ago are 'forgotten', because these memories are overtaken by even more horrific events. A slow escalation of crisis and anxiety can lead to numbness and despair.

But there can also be unity in this experience. We are still present and active actors in reality.

Don't give up. Find ways to use your voice, talents, and whatever privilege you can access to advance change.

Look for other change agents, especially in places or groups that might not be obvious allies at first glance. Harvey Milk connected union members together with the LGBTQ+ community, bringing people from both to successfully organize against discrimination.

Here are a few ways to stay connected along the way.

Subscribe to my email list and every few weeks you'll receive helpful tips, new approaches, occasional 'random-yet-humorous' stories, etc. I'm mindful of inbox overload, so you can opt-out and back in at any time. More details and an easy sign-up are available at PagingDrJen.com

This is also the best channel if you find yourself stuck or looking for someone to lead the charge into your company's next culture shift. I'm most frequently contacted to speak about, or help, companies envision/design/reclaim their workplace culture as a ~~consultant~~...erm...trusted guide.

Stay social. Follow me:

- LinkedIn at https://www.linkedin.com/in/jenoryan
- Twitter at @PagingDrJen
- Instagram at @PagingDrJen (TBH, this is mostly running events and pictures of my dog)

Lastly, you can also bookmark this helpful update page, PagingDrJen.com. This is a great way to get early access to expansion pack content and alerts for upcoming events.

And occasionally remind yourself that yes, you can. Change is possible AF.

*Art credit: Mike O'Connor.*
*We were just outside of Glasgow when the Neeps started to take hold.*

# Glossary

Organized by section. Check the resource section of PagingDrJen.com/IAF-updates for the latest information on any of these terms.

## *Introduction*

**LGBTQ+** – Lesbian, Gay, Bisexual, Transgender, and Queer or Questioning. The plus sign indicates the multitude of other identities.

**GSA** – Gay/Straight Alliance, also Gender and Sexuality Alliance. Youth clubs most often organized within the school system. Typically led by students with at least one faculty sponsor.

**Cisgender (also, cis)** – Self-identifying term. Describes a person whose gender identity aligns with the gender assigned to them at birth.

**Narrative – Red Pen**

> **Heteronormative** – Belief or unconscious assumption that being heterosexual is the default setting for humans. Example, using "Moms and Dads" instead of parents, or using only male/female couple in wedding examples. Shows up in language, images, research, customer personas, etc..

**Invisible Diversity** – Personal characteristics or attributes that include one in a marginalized population but are not immediately or easily observable. Example, a bisexual man might be assumed straight in the workplace if married to a woman. Invisible diversity highlights our reliance on stereotypes, assumptions, and observable traits to indicate or categorize diversity.

### Chapter One

**Baby Boomers** – The cohort of humans born from 1946-1964

**Generation X** – The cohort of humans born from 1965-1980

**Millennial** – The cohort of humans born from 1981-1996

### Chapter Three

**Gender Identity** – The innate sense of one's own gender.

**Transgender** – Self-identifying term. Describes a person whose gender identity is not aligned with the gender assigned to them at birth. Commonly used as an umbrella term to describe gender diverse or non-binary individuals.

**Non-Binary** – Self-identifying term. Describes a person who identifies outside of a female / male gender binary.

**Agender** – Self-identifying term. Describes a person who identifies as not having a specific gender.

**Gender-fluid** – Self-identifying term. Describes a person whose gender identity is dynamic, rather than being a single, discrete category.

**Orientation or Attraction** – Describes one's patterns of attraction. (gay, lesbian, asexual, bisexual, and so on.)

**Asexual** – Self-identifying term. Describes a person who doesn't experience sexual attraction.

**Non-binary indicator or marker** – Alternative to using only female or male options when specifying gender is necessary. Commonly used on state Issued identification cards or driver licenses. Can be displayed as "F", "M", or "X" options.

**Coming out** – Disclosing to others, or internally acknowledging, one's own sexual orientation or gender identity.

# References and Resources

### *Chapter One*

Community Marketing & Insights (CMI) (2017). 11th Annual LGBT Community Survey. Retrieved from https://cmi.info/lgbtq-research-downloads/#community-surveys

Community Marketing & Insights (CMI) (2018). 12th Annual LGB Q Community Survey. Retrieved from https://cmi.info/lgbtq-research-downloads/#community-surveys

Community Marketing & Insights (CMI) (2019). 13th Annual LGBTQ Community Survey. Retrieved from https://cmi.info/lgbtq-research-downloads/#community-surveys

Institute for Public Relations (IPR) (2016). Millennials@ Work: Perspectives on Diversity and Inclusion. Retrieved from https://instituteforpr.org/

BCG Henderson Institute (BCG) (2018). How Diverse Leadership Teams Boost Innovation. Retrieved from https://www.bcg.com/

Harvard Business Review (HBR) (2016). Diverse Teams Feel Less Comfortable – and That's Why They Perform Better. Retrieved from https://hbr.org/

MIT Sloan Executive Education Blog (MIT) (2017). What makes a high-performing team? The answer may surprise you. Retrieved from https://executive.mit.edu/

Human Rights Campaign Foundation (HRC) (2014). The Cost of the Closet and Rewards of Inclusion. Retrieved from https://hbr.org/

Human Rights Campaign Foundation (HRC) (2018). A Workplace Divided: Understanding the Climate of LGBTQ Workers Nationwide. Retrieved from https://hbr.org/

National Center for Transgender Equality (James et al., 2016). The Report of the 2015 U.S. Transgender Survey James, S. E., Herman, J. L., Rankin, S., Keisling, M., Mottet, L., & Anafi, M. (2016). Retrieved from https://transequality.org/

"A Beautiful Mind" from Universal Studios (2002). Directed by Ron Howard and based on the story of mathematician John Nash. (IMBD)

## Chapter Four

"This is Your Brain on Drugs" – 1987 Anti-Drug Commercial by Partnership for a Drug-Free America (aka Partnership at Drugfree.org) (available https://youtu.be/F0kCYP_iPtg)

Gudetama character credit to Sanrio. More information available on https://www.sanrio.com/

George Carlin IMDB (https://www.imdb.com/name/nm0137506/) Standup routine about driving available through multiple channels online.

## Chapter Five

Prepacked travel experiences are not recommended, but if you must, they are available at https://disneyworld.disney.go.com/

## Chapter Seven

Nordstrom – Press Release on 100% Pay Equity. (2019). Retrieved from https://press.nordstrom.com/

Accenture – Getting to Equal (goal of 50/50 by 2025). (2019). Retrieved from https://www.accenture.com/

AnitaB.org – "Tech Equity for All Women" (50/50 by 2025). (2019). Retrieved from https://anitab.org/

JAMA Pediatrics (JAMA) (2017). Difference-in-Differences Analysis of the Association Between State Same-Sex Marriage Policies and Adolescent Suicide Attempts. Retrieved from https://jamanetwork.com/

Centers for Disease Control (CDC) (2015). Youth Risk Behavior Surveillance System Data. Retrieved from https://www.cdc.gov/

GLAAD (GLADD) (2019). Accelerating Acceptance. Retrieved from https://www.glaad.org/

## Chapter Nine

Credit for the original O.P.P. goes to the phenomenal rap group, *Naughty by Nature*. And their 1991 smash hit. https://en.wikipedia.org/wiki/O.P.P._(song)

For a more up-to-date online list of resources, visit PagingDrJen.com/IAF-updates

*All links were accurate at the time of publication, August 2020.*

## About the Author

Dr. Jen O'Ryan is the founder and principal of Double Tall Consulting, specializing in the design of Inclusion and Diversity strategies. Leveraging two decades of experience in change management, Jen has guided organizations across a variety of industries through her process.

A data geek at heart, Jen brings an extensive grasp of how people interact with technology, with each other, and with change. She understands the challenges leaders face in promoting a truly inclusive and welcoming environment for their LGBTQ+ customers, clients, and employees.

Jen holds a PhD in Human Behavior, focused on gender identity and sexual orientation, as well as an MBA in Technology Management and B.A. in Ethics and Human Behavior.

Outside of I&D work, Jen is a travel enthusiast and avid runner. She has a strange affinity for bad 80's music, getting lost in new cities, and scary movies.

Jen frequently speaks on panels, conferences, and podcasts related to gender identity, sexual orientation, and influencing change across organizations. To connect with Jen, or learn more about her work, visit PagingDrJen.com or DoubleTallLLC.com.

CPSIA information can be obtained
at www.ICGtesting.com
Printed in the USA
BVHW052152220322
632091BV00014B/1011